The Complete Guide to Coarse Fisheries in the Irish Midlands

Acknowledgements

Many thanks to the following for all their kind help and advice: my wife Philomena and daughters Marianne and Fidelma for all their help and the following anglers who offered up photos – Peter Dillon, Tony Egan, Brian Bohan, David O'Malley, Tony Herbert, Joe McDermott and British anglers Peter Newton and Ian Young; to Brian Bohan and Tony Egan for all their invaluable help and advice.

Thanks to Max and Trevor for putting up with me on all those exploring fishing trips. To the members of the farming community, whom I have found to be always helpful and friendly, to Jim Baxter, editor of the British-based Angling Star magazine for all the help in promoting Book 1, to Matt Hayes, Sky News presenter and Angling Times correspondent for taking the time out to launch Book 1 at the Angling Show in Birmingham. Many thanks to Julian Grattidge who helped promote Book 1 on his excellent website www.anglersnet.co.uk

Thanks to all my advertisers, who have allowed me to invest more money in the marketing of Book 2, to Derek Rowley of Lakeland Fisheries for the kind foreword, to Mattie Nolan, Dr. Joe Caffrey, Fergal Lynch, Dermott Broughan, John Ryan and all the other members of the Shannon Fishery Board for their help and advice and the fish for restocking. Many thanks to the staff of Turner Print Group, especially Derek Creighton and Davey Foudy. A warm thanks to Keith Millar for the excellent production and design of Book 2, to Paddy Egan for his lovely poem depicting the demise of the corncrake and finally to my good friend Paddy for staying the course with me and being a constant source of ...

GW00503785

Front Cover

Top Left:	John Hand and Anthony Egan ... ids and some plump tench from L... ng Stones. This catch was taken d...
Top Right:	That's me releasing a nice tench into Lough Nabelwy, No. 23 in the Ten Stepping Stones.
Bottom Left:	Over 150lb of bream for Tony Egan during June 2004. This catch was taken from Lough Doogary, No. 24 in the Ten Stepping Stones. Note the golden colour around the fishes mouth.
Bottom Right:	Trevor, an English angler, with this lovely streamlined Irish Midland pike.

Contents

Contents

The Corncrake

by Paddy Egan

It's over forty summers now since I heard her lonesome crake,
When the landrails morning chorus used to keep me wide awake,
In cornfields and in meadows she lived and reared her brood
Now the corncrake's voice is silent, in fact she's gone for good.

In years gone by the farmers mowed their meadows from the middle of July
So the corncrake and the partridge had time to hatch and fly
But we finished with haymaking when the silage came along
Now the hum of forage harvesters has replaced the corncrake's song.

The use of pesticides and weedkillers have also made their contribution
And the over use of fertilisers are causing land pollution,
They have got alarmed in Brussels but they don't know where to start
In trying to save our birdlife they've put the horse behind the cart.

Down along the Shannon's banks a few corncrakes have survived
And they're prepared to spend a fortune to keep those precious birds alive
But the odds are stacked against them as they try to save them from annihilation
With just a score of birds remaining they face a desperate situation.

But the corncrake's not the only bird about whose survival we concern
There's the curlew and the lapwing, the partridge, owl, and tern
There's so many on the danger list that give reason for alarm
We no longer hear them calling as we work upon the farm.

There were birds of prey who slept by day and hunted through the night
They caught mice and rats in one fell swoop with x-ray vision sight,
We had game birds in the meadows like partridge, grouse and plover
But like our friend the corncrake those birds are gone forever.

In days of yore around Glanmore there were birds of every feather,
Where the farmer and the wildlife had learned to live together,
We have played our part there is no doubt in our bird elimination
And the corncrake will no longer wake our rural population.

FISHING TACKLE SHOPS

Lakeland Fishery

Lakeland Fishery is located 1km from the picturesque village of Roosky, on the border of counties Roscommon, Longford and Leitrim. Roosky is just an hour and a half from Dublin on the N4, and an hour from Sligo.

Lakeland Fishery is set in 20 acres and provides everything for the discerning angler in beautiful and peaceful settings, with the opportunity to catch most species including carp, tench, rudd, hybrid, roach and bream. The fishery offers fishing for quality fish and another dimension to fishing in Ireland.

There are three mature lakes – Kingfisher, Mallard and Heron, one of which overlooks one of the best River Shannon weir pools that simply begs to be fished.

Lakeland Fishery has a car park area, separate male and female toilets. A fully stocked tackle shop, Maver, Trabucco and Brilo, etc which will supply you with all your requirements.

The fishery is owned and maintained by Irish International Derek Rowley. The lakes are constantly monitored to ensure quality fish and stocking levels.

Opening Times

Summer
9.00am – 9.00pm

Winter
9.00am – Dusk

DAY TICKET FISHERY

Phone:
00-353-(0)71 9638463

Mobile:
00-353-(0)87 6178190

Email:
derek@lakelandfishery.com

Website:
www.lakelandfishery.com

Ireland's Premier Fishery

FOREWORD

AFTER reading Bernie's first book, I was looking forward to Book No. 2. Well, to say it has been worth the wait is an understatement.

This second helping covers 52 fisheries from Leitrim into Longford and onto Cavan. Once again he has captured some interesting photographs and used detailed maps to assist the angler in getting to the venues.

I thoroughly enjoyed Bernie's adventures with Paddy and I hope that one day I might have an opportunity to meet the elusive Paddy.

Once you start reading this book you will appreciate how much time and effort Bernie has put into this project, including locating and visiting the fisheries, plotting the depth and talking with anglers in relation to the best methods of fishing each venue.

These angling guides are a great aid in the promotion of angling in the Irish Midlands as they not only provide invaluable information on fishing in this area but also give the reader a wonderful insight into life in rural Ireland.

I am eagerly awaiting the third book in the series.

Derek Rowley
Irish International

The shaded area represents the area of the Irish Midlands covered in this series of five books.

Ireland

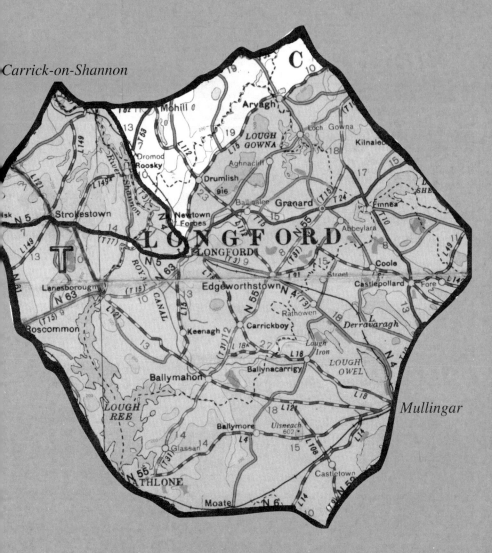

Outlined in this map is the area of the Irish Midlands I will be covering in this series of five books. I have lightened the two areas I will be covering in Book 2: The Ten Stepping Stones and The Breffni Quarter.

TOOMAN FARMHOUSE ACCOMMODATION

Travelling from Dublin to Tooman House take the N4 Dublin to Sligo Road, six miles from Longford town (on the Sligo side) turn at the Tooman House road sign and follow the country road for four miles to Tooman House.

We cater for all the visiting anglers needs. All rooms en-suite with tea and coffee making facilities. The best of home cooking in a family atmosphere. Lunch boxes and flasks available at small extra cost. Local pubs with live music most nights. Our shop in site offers a full range of bait and tackle. Boats for hire and angling information always available.

TOOMAN ANGLING & LEISURE

When in the Carrick-on-Shannon area, do call around to our shop – just beside the bridge. We stock all your requirements – fishing tackle, bait, ground baits, waders, wellingtons and clothing. Tony will be delighted to meet you, and give friendly tips and advice on angling in this area.

INTRODUCTION

The Book's Layout

W**ELCOME** along to my second book in this series of five guide books covering coarse fishing in the Irish Midlands.

I hope you enjoyed your journey through Book 1. The format in Book 2 will be similar to my first book, with all the old favourites present as well as a few extra stories about my own and Paddy's adventures over the years. These stories have proved very popular. I have also included some of my thoughts on the Fishery Board and angling tourism. I do not want to sound political in what is basically a guide book. However, I feel that what I have written needs to be said if our wild coarse fisheries are to survive and prosper in the coming years.

I must say I am delighted with the positive way my first book has been received. This has been a great source of encouragement for me to carry on with this series of five guide books and also to add new features. In this regard, I would like to thank you the reader.

In Book 2 I have allowed a limited amount of advertising. The money from these adverts will be used to market the book. I have found that marketing can prove very expensive and as the profits from the book are so small, it takes a lot of sales just to cover the advertising costs. In this regard, I would like to encourage the readers to support my advertisers where possible.

The proceeds from this series of five books will be going to the following three charities – **Longford Hospice Home Care**, **Save the Otter** and **Our Lady's Hospital for Sick Children**. Paddy and myself thought this over and decided together on the three charities that will benefit from the sales of the books.

If I have one regret from my first book, it was the way I was over enthusiastic in my praise of certain fisheries. This enthusiasm was based on my experience of fishing these lakes some years previous to the book's publication. For some reason, which I try to explain later on in the book, these fisheries were not fishing as well as I had predicted. Having said that, from reports during 2004 it seems they have improved. In this book, where possible, I have tried to get up-to-date information as well as photographic evidence on the fisheries.

On our journey to the fifty-two lakes in Book 2 we will be travelling through three counties – Leitrim, Longford and Cavan. I am going to stick my neck out and say that I genuinely believe that this part of the Irish Midlands is a mecca for the coarse angler. Thankfully, this statement is based on up-to-date evidence. What has surprised me most is the amount of fabulous tench, bream, rudd and pike fishing on offer. Having said that, these are wild Irish fish who see very little in the way of anglers – it will take experience and perseverance to attract them and then trick them into taking your hook bait.

Since the publication of Book 1, I have purchased a fish finder – the make is an *Eagle Trifinder.* I have found this instrument very useful in finding out the depths of the various lakes which I have passed on. As regards identifying fish shoals, if the fish finder is accurate then the lakes I have visited in this book are well stocked with fish. However, one feature that has stood out on most of the lakes is the way the shoals of fish are mainly concentrated out in the middle of the lake in the deeper water and lying near the bottom.

I have also purchased an electric boat engine, after nearly forty years of rowing a boat – I think I deserve the comfort this affords me. I find the engine a great way of getting around the lakes and being electric it is very quiet. On a full charge I get up to four hours, which is more than adequate for a day's fishing – just in case, I keep my oars close at hand!

Call it coincidence or divine intervention, but for some reason things have happened which I had not planned and have proven beneficial to Book 2. A few examples of this was first Glasshouse Lough – on my first visit I went to a different lake thinking it was Glasshouse. I wrote about this lake for my book. Just by chance I decided to call back with my fish finder to get some depths. When I arrived I found the gate into the lake was locked, so I turned around and started to head for home. On my way up the road I meet a local man on a bike. By chance I decided to ask him if he knew any other way into Glasshouse Lough. He told me that the lake I was visiting was not Glasshouse and that it was further up the road and in to the right. So there you have it, I was very nearly sending the readers to the wrong lake.

I was planning to publish this second book before the end of 2003. One night in early November I was looking at my video which I am making to complement Book 2 when I noticed what I thought was a wooden platform on the far bank of Gartinardress. In my report on this lake I put it down as a fishery with no shorefishing and definitely a lake for the exploring angler. When the opportunity arose I drove out as far as Gartinardress to check it out. During my searching in a wooded area on the far bank, I found not one but three well-built wooden platforms. At this stage I decided to leave publication over until the following spring, just in case some new information that would be of help to visiting anglers might become available.

During May 2004, when I was working flat out to get the book published, another bit of divine intervention came my way. I decided to travel up as far as Lough Aduff and Errill to put up my advertising posters. For some reason on my way home I decided to call around by Lough Cloonfinnan. When I arrived at Cloonfinnan I met with a local Leitrim angler by the name of Brian Bohan and was eager to get his views on lakes in this area. After an interesting chat I presented Brian with Book 1 and gave him my phone number, telling him I would soon be publishing Book 2, and asking him to let me know if he managed to have a good catch on some of the local lakes.

It was, I think, the last Saturday in May. I had just arrived home from a fishing trip when the phone rang. It was Brian – he told me he had a good catch of tench on Cloonfinnan and if I could call over to see them within the next hour he would wait on. Lucky enough I was free to make the journey and you can see the evidence on the back page. Since then, Brian has been invaluable in helping me with up-to-date information on the fishing on Loughs Errill, McHugh, Drumbad and Rinn.

Another angler, Tony Egan, and his son Tony Jr, from the north Longford area have also been invaluable in passing on information on Loughs Doogary, Sallagh and Gortermone. Photographs of this evidence are also featured in Book 2.

As I am writing these notes, it is now Monday, 16th August 2004. I hope to have Book 2 going to press before the end of the month. However, I am still wondering to myself what new bit of information will come my way before then.

Finally, to finish off this introduction, I would ask visiting anglers to have respect for local landowners. In most cases we rely on the goodwill of the farming community to get to the lakes. It's very important that we respect this goodwill and make sure to close all gates, leave no litter lying about, and where possible ask permission from the local landowner.

New Thoughts on Coarse Fishing in the Irish Midlands

DURING October 2002, a few months after the publication of my first book, I received an interesting email from a British angler by the name of Jeff Edwards.

Jeff and a friend spent a week coarse fishing during the month of June 2002 around the Strokestown area. Despite putting in plenty of effort they experienced, to put it mildly, very poor fishing. Jeff was particularly disappointed with Lough Patrick, which he and his friend had fished on three consecutive days and could only manage to catch one small pike. This was Jeff's first visit to this part of the Irish Midlands, and he wanted to know why the fishing was so bad. I emailed Jeff and told him I would give serious thought to the matter and try and uncover the reasons for the poor fishing.

The first and most obvious thing that came to mind was the fact that the spring and summer of 2002 was one of the coldest and wettest on record. With temperatures so low, I thought this might be one of the reasons why the fish were not in taking mood. There were also reports that due to the low temperature during spring and early summer the coarse fish stocks might have become spawn bound, also during 2002 the very wet weather had caused widespread flooding, leaving wooden platforms and adjacent fields under water. Might the fish have moved to these new pastures to feed?

Another thought that came to mind – could there be some form of pollution finding its way into our waterways that is having an effect on the fish? Or could some natural disease have set in to the fish stocks? Here in the Irish Midlands there have been reports of illegal netting of our lakes and rivers, could this be behind the fall in fish numbers?

Zebra Mussels – Lough Nablahy

Recently here in Ireland there has been a lot of talk about zebra mussels, and how they are becoming widespread in our lakes and rivers. To be honest, I know very little about this recent visitor to Ireland. I have been told the effect they

have on a river or lake is to make the water crystal clear. As fish, in particular bream and tench, love to keep to the shade, then these fish, as water levels fall, might be moving about from swim to swim and lake to lake in order to find suitable cover. As most of the lakes here in the Irish Midlands are joined together by small rivers, this movement of fish is quite easy. If this is the case, then one can see why the angler is finding it hard to meet up with the shoals of fish.

During the summer of 2003 I received reports that the fishing on Lough Nablahy was, to be honest, crap. However, in the month of September the fishing suddenly exploded on this lake, with anglers catching loads of big bream, tench, rudd, hybrids and pike.

Where did all the fish come from? I can only guess that they were off in some of the other lakes that lie close by and can be easily negotiated by small rivers. Why did they return to Nablahy during the autumn? Once again, it's guess work on my part. Unlike 2002, the summer of 2003 was very hot and dry causing low water levels. Might the fish shoals have moved back to Nablahy where the water goes down to a depth of seventy feet? Another thought, could the local fish stocks use Nablahy because of its depth as an overwintering lake?

In July 2002 I met up with a British angler who had a good catch of large bream from Lough Cloonfinnan. I was delighted to have the evidence in photo form which is on page 70. With requests coming in from visiting anglers on good places to fish, I sent some of them to Cloonfinnan, however, when I received emails back they told me they could catch no fish on this lake.

In May 2004 I received a mobile phone call from local Leitrim angler Brian Bohan telling me he was on the shore of Lough Cloonfinnan and had a great catch of tench, and if I called over I could get a photo and do some videoing.

It was around 6.00pm on a Saturday evening and when I arrived at the lake I found Brian with two keep nets full of tench. He had fished right through the night from 6.00pm on Friday to 6.00pm on Saturday. Brian's catch which were taken on a ledgered maggot and worm combination consisted of twenty-eight tench ranging from 3lbs to 7lbs and one large bream (see photo on back cover).

It has to be said that Brian is a very knowledgeable angler, and knows the local lakes like the back of his hand. He had ground baited his swim each day for a week with his own BB special mix. A few days prior to his visit there was a

heavy day's rain, which after a long dry spell had freshened up the water and on the day before he started to fish the temperature had risen by about three degrees Celsius.

In recent years one of the most puzzling questions is the fall off in the numbers of bream being caught here in the Irish Midlands. During early June 2004 I heard reports of local north Longford angler Tony Egan having a great bream session on Lough Doogary.

When I met up with Tony, another very knowledgeable angler he told me he had taken over 150lb of bream in one session on Doogary. At the time, I had written about this lake for my second book, and I described it as a lake for exploring anglers which looked like it had great potential.

Tony brought me over to Peter Dillon's Pub in Ballinamuck where he showed me a photo of the catch, which can be seen on the front cover. What makes this catch of bream even more puzzling was the fact that Tony had done no previous ground baiting. Seemingly the shoal moved into his swim and Tony managed to keep them there. The successful method was ledgering maggot with the feeder and plenty of baiting of his swim. Depending on temperatures, it is around this time of year that wild Irish bream take time out to spawn. Might Tony have hit upon a shoal that had recently spawned and were now very hungry and in search of food?

During July 2004, I decided to call over to Hollybank Lake to get a photo of the shore line. When I arrived I met up with Lanesboro angler Pat Mulryan and his son. They were having a great bream session – beside them were two British anglers who were also enjoying a good days fishing for bream. This was around midday which is an unusual time to find the bream in a feeding mood. The water along their shoreline was very green in colour – could the darkness of the water have tricked the bream into feeding during the day?

I believe there are a lot of secrets surrounding the behaviour of wild Irish fish, and it will take the dedicated and thoughtful angler to uncover these mysteries. After over forty years of fishing, I am still listening, observing and above all, learning about the movements and feeding habits of wild Irish fish. This, for me, is what makes angling here in the Irish Midlands such a fascinating hobby.

Angling Tourism

First of all, let me say as I write these notes I have no business interests as regards angling tourism. However, for the people who do — fishing tackle shops, bait suppliers, bed and breakfast accommodation, restaurants, pubs and angling holiday operators — if they are to continue to attract anglers to the Irish Midlands, then they will have to take a more active role in the protection and improvement of our coarse fisheries.

I believe the best way to achieve this is to lobby the people in government with responsibility for angling tourism to give a realistic funding to the Fishery Boards to enable them to carry out an extensive restocking programme. The increase in fish numbers should be the top priority, in particular pike, bream and tench.

The improvement of access to the fisheries is also very important. I have noticed a lot of regular visiting anglers who have fished in this area for quite a long time and are now getting on in age and need easy access, especially while carrying a lot of fishing gear.

I don't mean all the lakes should have easy access, with well built wooden platforms. The thought of a wild fishery, which because of the difficulty in getting to it sees very little in the way of anglers is the type of fishery that has great appeal to some anglers, particularly the younger and more adventurous fishermen.

Years ago, Ireland was very fortunate in being the only real angling destination for British coarse anglers. However, in this age of cheap air travel, anglers have now a wide range of countries to visit. The most popular of these are Denmark, Holland and France.

From being a country who could sit back and enjoy the income from visiting anglers, we now have to face keen competition from other European countries. In this regard, we are losing out badly, mainly due to the fact that we have invested very little in the protection and improvement of our natural wild fisheries. In fact, in recent years the government have cut back the funding to the Fishery Boards, which to me shows a total disregard for this section of Irish tourism.

When one considers that there are reported to be close on five million coarse anglers in Britain, which is more than the total population of Ireland, then the lack of interest shown by the government is all the more puzzling.

As I said in my first book, here in the Irish Midlands, we have very little in the way of tourist attractions. Our biggest asset is our wild Irish coarse fisheries. At present the government are treating this section of Irish tourism as a joke – if they continue down this path, then they can expect more and more foreign anglers to treat it in the same way.

Andy Gadulski, a regular visiting angler from Buckinghamshire in England. Andy is enjoying a day's fishing along the Royal Canal at Abbeyshrule. (Hope I got the name right – Bernie)

Fishery Board and Restocking

One solution that I thought might be of help in improving coarse fishing here in the Irish Midlands was to restock local lakes. I heard a report that the Fishery Board were busy netting coarse fish in local trout fisheries, so I decided to get in touch with Mattie Nolan, Inspector of the Shannon Fishery Board, with a view to getting some of these coarse fish transferred to lakes here in the Irish Midlands. When I phoned Mattie, he told me as soon as fish became available he would send some of his staff with them to a lake of my choice.

During April 2003, Mattie phoned to let me know he had some nice tench and rudd that were removed from Lough Owel, and where would I like them transferred to? I picked out Lough Drimmon, a nice coarse fishery which is situated up near Strokestown in Co. Roscommon.

When the Fishery Board arrived at Drimmon I was absolutely delighted with the quality of the fish (photo on page 15). There was close on 300 tench and rudd released into Drimmon. Directions to Lough Drimmon are on page 48 of Book 1.

More large tench

After this initial restocking I phoned to thank Mattie and his staff for the fish, and asked that when any further fish became available could he keep me in mind? It was June 2004 when Mattie got back with the news that he had close on 400 large tench which were removed from Lough Owel and asked where would I like them transferred to.

On this occasion, I decided to distribute the fish into three fisheries in the Leitrim, Cavan, north Longford area – Loughs Keeldra, Nabelwy and Sallagh. There was close on 200 put into Keeldra and Nabelwy with the remaining 200 going into Lough Sallagh. These fish weighed between 2lbs and 6lbs and were ready to spawn so hopefully they will have settled into their new homes and increase in number and size over the coming years.

In the context of all of the lakes here in the Irish Midlands, I know this restocking is on a small scale, however, I believe it's a start in the right direction and if you are reading this Mattie, how about some nice bream and maybe a few carp. Hoping to hear from you soon! Bernie.

NOTE:

Just before the publication of this book, I had a chat with Mattie Nolan. He told me the Fishery Board had suspended gill netting of pike. This is good news for the pike angler. Mattie said they were looking into other methods of removing pike from prime trout fisheries.

One method which I think is a great idea, is to allow pike fishing competitions on these lakes and after weigh-in, the pike are then transferred alive to stock coarse fisheries.

Mattie also had good news regarding the stocking of carp into lakes here in the Irish Midlands. He said the Fishery Board are planning in the near future to identify suitable lakes for carp. At present France is doing a huge tourist trade through visiting carp anglers. In the future, the Irish Midlands might be able to compete with France for the ever growing number of carp anglers in Britain.

Members of the Shannon Fishery Board restocking Lough Drimmon, a lake from my first book. On this occasion they released 300 quality tench and rudd into the lake. Pictured (left to right) are: Sean Scanlon, Fergal Lynch, Gerry Walshe, Mr Brennan – landowner and Andrew Cullen.

A WEE CHAT – 'BERNIE AND PADDY'

Bernie: Well Paddy, it's great to see you, are you still with me as we venture into Book 2.

Paddy: Bernie it's my pleasure and an honour to be involved as we journey through your second book.

Bernie: Does that mean you will allow me to take your photo and maybe pass on a bit more information on your good self to the readers.

Paddy: The decision I made to stay private was, I believe, the best one for me. Since the publication of your first book, I have seen how busy you have become going to meetings, travelling to angling shows, all that e-mailing and meeting up with fellow anglers. Bernie, I hope you will respect my need for privacy and still allow me to be involved with you in Book 2.

Bernie: Paddy, ever since that time in the late nineteen seventies when you retreated to that old quarry to allow yourself time to regain your peace of mind. I have always respected your need for privacy. For this journey through Book 2, its my pleasure and honour to have you along.

Paddy: Thanks for the kind words, I only hope I can be of some help. Bernie, I was wondering about Book 1, were you happy with the way it was received?

Bernie: As it was my first time to write a book, I had a lot of fears as regards how it would be accepted by fellow anglers. In this regard I am delighted with the response I have received which has given me great encouragement to continue with Book 2.

Paddy: Bernie, you mentioned to me on numerous occasions the importance of marketing and how you find this so difficult and time consuming. Have you learned much from your experience of Book 1.

Bernie: I have found in this day and age for something to be really successful, as well as being a good product, it also needs plenty of marketing. In this regard, my budget was so small that I could not make any real impact with my advertising campaign. In fact Paddy, to be honest, I spent money on advertising which I now know was foolish on my part.

Paddy: Do you reckon Bernie you will be a wiser man on the marketing front when it comes to Book 2.

Bernie: Well Paddy experience is a good teacher. The profit margin on the book is so small that the cost of advertising can often prove more expensive than the

revenue earned on the sale of the book. This is particularly so in Britain where I have to pay in Sterling. I have to be extremely selective where I place advertisements. In this regard I would be hoping for some advice and help from the tourist sector. Here in Ireland visiting anglers are a very important part of the tourist industry and I would like to think that my book does its part in promoting this side of tourism in the Irish Midlands.

On the subject of marketing, I am hoping to get my books into Waterstones bookshops throughout the British Isles and Easons here in Ireland. So if readers or their friends are looking for extra books then call around to your local Waterstone or Easons bookshop. If the book is not in stock, you might ask them to order it for you.

Paddy: When you published Book 1 in 2002, the spring and summer of that year were very wet and cold and most visiting anglers experienced poor fishing. What impact did this have on your book?

Bernie: Yes Paddy I could not have picked a worse year to launch my first guidebook onto the angling market. I think the summer of 2002 went down as the wettest and coldest on record. Visiting anglers had a horrid time of it with lakes flooded out onto nearby fields leaving wooden stands under water. However, anglers are a resilient bunch and most of them would know that this was a once off as was proved during 2003, when we had a much drier and warmer spring and summer.

Paddy: Knowing what you know now is there anything you might have changed in Book 1?

Bernie: Overall Paddy I am very pleased with the way Book 1 has turned out and I would like to thank you for all your kind help. If I have one regret I think I was a bit over enthusiastic with my reports on some lakes. It was a number of years since I had fished these lakes and my report was based on past experience. However, in recent years it seems for some reason stocks of fish in these lakes have declined. Why this should be so I'm not sure.

Paddy: Are you still planning to donate the proceeds of the book to charity?

Bernie: I have decided Paddy that the proceeds from this series of five books will go to the following three charities:
• **Longford Hospice for Home Care**
• **Save the Otter**, which is nearly extinct in the Irish Midlands
• **Our Lady's Hospital for Sick Children in Dublin**

Paddy: Bernie that's very kind of you and I am delighted with the idea.

Bernie: However, from the sales of my first book I did use money to purchase various items. These included an electric engine, battery and charger, fish finder, digital camera and a video camera which, at present, I am using to make a video of Book 2. I feel if I find something that will enable me to improve the books then I should purchase it.

Paddy: That sounds fair enough.

Bernie: Paddy is there anything you would like to comment on?

Paddy: Respect for the fish, animals and birds that we encounter. Recently, I came upon a water hen who was in a terrible state of distress, the poor birds legs were caught up in fishing line. Lucky enough I came upon her in time and was able to free her before much damage was done. I would like to ask your readers to make sure not to leave any fishing line lying about. Recently, I heard a story about a group of six visiting pike anglers who were over in the Irish Midlands on a week's holiday. After their morning's fishing trip they would take one pike each and do the same after their evening's fishing trip. If you add the amount of fish they took over the course of their week's holidays it will come to a lot of pike. To counteract this plundering of our pike stocks, I think there should be a total ban on anglers killing pike.

Bernie: Paddy, I agree with you on both points.

Paddy: At this stage in our evolution, we have become masters of the planet. I believe God will judge us not on how big a car we drive, the house we live in or how expensive a holiday we can afford but on how well we cared for and respected the fellow creatures that also inhabit this planet.

Bernie: I must say Paddy I agree wholeheartedly with what you have said.

Paddy: You know Bernie that story you wrote on fly-fishing on the Camlin River, I was hoping that you might include it in this book.

Bernie: You are afraid you might not be around when I decide to write a book on game fishing in the Irish Midlands.

Paddy: Now you have it Bernie.

Bernie: This book is a coarse fishing guide however, Paddy as a favour to you I will include the story on fly fishing.

Paddy: Bernie many thanks and I am really looking forward to this coarse fishing journey through the Irish Midlands.

Bernie: Is there anything else Paddy before we move on.

Paddy: Yes Bernie – would this be a good time to go for a few pints.

Bernie: No way Paddy we have too much work in front of us.

GONE FISHING!

Map of Area 3

To Carrick-on-Shannon

To Cloone

MOHILL

To Arvagh

ROOSKY

DRUMLISH

ARVAGH

LONGFORD

1	L. Gortinty	
2	L. Aduff	
3	L. Mucklaghan	
4	L. McHugh	
5	L. Errill	
6	L. Cloonfinnan	
7	L. Bog	
8	L. Cloonturk	
9	L. Cloonboniagh	
10	L. Gubagraffy	
11	L. Roosky	
12	L. Drumard	
13	L. Rinn	
14	L. Creenagh	
15	L. Sallagh (1)	
16	L. Errew	
17	L. Drumbad	
18	L. Drumshanbo	
19	L. Keeldra	
20	L. Sallagh (2)	
21	L. Fearglass	
22	L. Clooncose	
23	L. Nabelwy	
24	L. Doogary	
25	L. Corglass	
26	L. Gortermone	
27	L. Tully	
28	L. Beaghmore	
29	L. Annagh	
30	L. Black	
31	L. Gulladoo	
32	L. Mullandarragh	
33	L. Town	
34	L. Gangin	
35	L. Mosy's	
36	L. Hollybank	

The Ten Stepping Stones

An Anglers Guide to Coarse Fisheries in the Irish Midlands

AREA 3

The Ten Stepping Stones

On our journey into Area 3 we must head eastwards and cross over the mighty River Shannon. I hope you found our previous journeys in Book 1, through the Golden Triangle and Paddy's Country, interesting and informative. I am calling Area 3 *The Ten Stepping Stones,* if you look closely at the map you will notice ten lakes, starting with Drumshanbo and finishing up with Gulladoo, travelling from left to right, representing Ten Stepping Stones.

This area is a real gem for the coarse fisherman. It offers up a tremendous variety and quality of fishing. There is the Bog Lake, which nestles inside a lovely wooded area where peace and quiet are the order of the day, and the bream and tench reign supreme. Next, we have one of Paddy's favourites, Cloonfinnan, where the pike grow big, feeding on the large bream and tench which are present in this heavily weeded fishery.

The largest lake in Area 3 is Rinn Lough where the fabulous Rinn House and gardens were built on its east shore. This is a noted coarse fishery and definitely one for the short list – Rinn offers up bream, rudd, roach, hybrid, perch, eel and tench fishing, and is noted for its big pike – there are also wild brown trout in this delightful fishery. Not far from Rinn Lough is Drumbad a mysterious lake, which nestles inside a mixed forest of conifers and broad-leafed trees – here the tench fisherman could realise his wildest dreams.

On a wildfowling trip back in the late 1960s, Paddy discovered the secrets of Lough Sallagh and its fabulous bream fishing. We have the three sister lakes – Gortermone, Tully and Beaghmore – which lie close together and can all be negotiated by boat via a small river. These three lakes offer up plenty of easy shore fishing to big pike, tench and bream, and of course the rest of the Ten Stepping Stones – all exciting fisheries for the coarse angler. There's many more jewels to visit, thirty-six in all, so let us get started on our journey.

Here is the order in which we will be visiting each fishery:

1. Lough Gortinty
2. Lough Aduff
3. Lough Mucklaghan
4. Lough McHugh
5. Lough Errill
6. Lough Cloonfinnan
7. Lough Bog
8. Lough Cloonturk
9. Lough Cloonboniagh
10. Lough Gubagraffy
11. Lough Roosky
12. Lough Drumard
13. Lough Rinn
14. Lough Creenagh
15. Lough Sallagh (1)
16. Lough Errew
17. Lough Clooncoe or Drumbad
18. Lough Drumshanbo
19. Keeldra Lake
20. Sallagh Lake (2)
21. Fearglass Lough
22. Clooncose Lake
23. Lough Nabelwy
24. Doogary Lough
25. Corglass Lough
26. Gortermone Lough
27. Tully Lough
28. Beaghmore Lake
29. Annagh Lake
30. Black Lake
31. Gulladoo Lough Upr and Lwr
32. Mullandaragh Lough
33. Town or Carrigallen Lough
34. Gangin Lough
35. Mosy's Lough
36. Lower Lough or Hollybank

Directions on "How to get there"

For lakes one to seventeen in Area 3, we will be using the bridge at Roosky on the N4 Longford to Carrick-on-Shannon road as the starting-off point (photo on page 67), while for directions to lakes eighteen to thirty-six, the starting-off point will be the crossroads in Drumlish village. Always remember we will be approaching these two starting-off points from the Longford road.

Gortinty Lake (1)

For our first lake, we must journey into lovely Leitrim to visit an excellent coarse fishery. Gortinty is a darkish lake with plenty of easy shore fishing. It holds stocks of rudd, roach, bream, tench, perch, and can also throw up 20lb+ pike. It was only in recent years, when I started to study maps to find out the locations of various lakes, that I first realised Gortinty was a large lake in its own right and not part of the Shannon system.

Verdict

Gortinty lies adjacent to the main N4 Carrick-on-Shannon road – there is easy access to plenty of comfortable shore fishing which is weed-free. This area can be most productive with mainly roach and bream, especially if it has been previously ground baited. I have had some nice pike fishing from my boat *Adventurer*. However, you will also get plenty of good pike fishing from the extensive shoreline. Gortinty is well worth a visit, especially if you are tight on time. There is also an area for launching boats. (Photo on page 76 of visiting British anglers on shore of Gortinty.)

How to get there

Approaching from the Longford road, when you meet the Roosky Bridge, you head straight on out the N4 Carrick-on-Shannon road for 6.3 miles, passing through Dromad village on the way. Gortinty lake is on your left. At this point there is plenty of shore fishing into eight to ten feet of water. If you don't mind walking a little journey along the shore of the lake, there is some excellent shore fishing up to the right past little island – here the depth is averaging seven feet. Just before you meet the lake there is a narrow road up to your left, if you drive up this road for 0.3 of a mile you will see a wooden stile on your right, down this field you will see more easy shore fishing. At its deepest, around the middle of the lake, Gortinty goes down to a depth of twenty-eight feet. Best of luck.

Fitting on the electric engine as I am about to head off for a days pike fishing in my boat *Adventurer*. Lough Gortinty offers up loads of easy shore fishing.

Lough Aduff (2)

This fishery lies just outside Carrick-on-Shannon of the N4 road, with a total of seven wooden platforms to fish from – Lough Aduff caters very well for the visiting angler. Despite my best intentions I have still to fish Aduff. From reports I have received from visiting British anglers, it seems it is mainly a tench fishery, with bream, roach, hybrids, perch, pike and eels also present.

Verdict
Congrats to the Fishery Board for all those wooden stands – it gives the opportunity to fish a large area of the shoreline. Lough Aduff is a dark fishery – I would recommend it for a visit, particularly if you were part of a large group of visiting anglers. On a visit to Lough Aduff during May of 2004, I met up with two Dublin anglers who were fishing off the two stands in front of a small river. Photo on page 77. They were having a good days fishing of the pole, with bream, roach, hybrids and perch to the fore. A pike close to the 20lb mark attacked a roach as he was near to being landed. Put Aduff on your short list.

How to get there
Approaching from the Longford road, when you meet the Roosky Bridge, you head straight out the N4 Carrick-on-Shannon road for 6.8 miles, passing through Dromad village on the way. At this point you take a right turn, and head down this road for just about fifty metres. Turn left here and go down this road for about 100 metres, where you will see a gate on the right with a wooden stile. To get to the lake you cross this stile, head up along pass in field and go through the gap in the hedge – you must now head over the hill where you will see the lake in front of you. Walk on down the hill till you meet a small wooden bridge at the river. To find the first four wooden platforms, keep on down to your left (do not cross the bridge). For the next three stands, you now have to cross a bridge, go on over to the second wooden bridge, you must cross here where you will find two wooden stands. For the final platform you head on up to the hedge, go through the gap in the hedge, and stand is

just in on your left. You will be fishing into between five and six feet of water. During very wet weather the stands on Lough Aduff can become flooded. Tight Lines.

Netting the catch is this Dublin angler on Lough Aduff. Note the well-built wooden stands.

Lough Mucklaghan (3)

We are now visiting a lake with very little shore fishing. Lough Mucklaghan offers up only one wooden stand, which is in a very precarious condition, and the visiting angler would be well advised to be very careful while using it. There is also the remnants of another stand, which has almost rotted away. I have never fished this lake, but I have that old fisherman's feeling it could well offer up some nice bream and tench fishing.

Verdict

This is quite a small fishery – the best bet for enjoying a day's fishing on Mucklaghan would be in a rubber dinghy. It is a very dark lake and has an extensive covering of lily pads around most of its shoreline. While on a visit, for the purposes of this book, I met some French anglers who were fishing from rubber dinghies – they told me they had caught some nice pike, with the heaviest weighing in at 20lbs 3ozs.

How to get there

Approaching from the Longford road, you drive straight on past the bridge at Roosky, and carry on out the N4 Carrick-on-Shannon road, passing through Dromod village on the way. When you have travelled 7.0 miles, you will see the Mohill road to your right with a sign for Lough McHugh. Go along this road for one mile where you will see a road to your left with a fishing sign, go up this road for 0.2 of a mile. At this point there is a gap in to the lake on your right (opposite the gate at house). Once again, if you manage to fish this lake, please let me know how you get on.

NOTE:

During June of 2004, I heard a report that Lough Mucklaghan was stocked with brown trout. At the time of going to print, I am still waiting for confirmation.

This visiting British angler fishing off the only wooden stand on Lough Mucklaghan. I have never fished this lake, but I have a feeling it could be a top class bream, tench and pike fishery.

Lough McHugh (4)

I have to admit, I have been planning to fish Lough McHugh, but like with so many other lakes here in the Irish Midlands, I still have not got around to it. On a visit for the purposes of this book in November 2003, I took my boat *Adventurer* out onto the lake, mainly to find out the various depths, and also to check out areas for shore fishing, wooden platforms, and of course where the shoals of fish are located. I must say if my fishfinder, an *Eagle Trifinder* is accurate, then this fishery holds a lot of fish, with some very big individuals also present. I have a feeling this is a top class coarse fishery.

Verdict

McHugh is a joy for the visiting angler, with loads of easy shore fishing into weed-free water, and four well-built wooden platforms. As soon as the opportunity arises, hopefully during 2004, myself and Paddy are planning a visit to this fishery. If we manage to get there before this book is published, then I will let you know how we got on. There were three areas of the lake that showed up large concentrations of fish. The first, was around the small island; second, in a small bay on the opposite side of the lake and the third, was down the middle of the lake, where some big fish showed up near the bottom of this exciting fishery. At the first stand near the parking area, you will be fishing into six to eight feet of water. For the other three stands, which are located in the next field up to the left, the lake quickly shelves off to between ten to fourteen feet. Out behind the little island, McHugh goes down to a depth of twenty feet, while out in the middle of the lake you will find the deepest point at twenty-eight feet.

This is the view you will see of Lough McHugh just in from the parking area. Note the wooden stands to the left of the island.

How to get there

Approaching from the Longford road, you drive straight on past the bridge in Roosky, and carry on out the N4 Carrick-on-Shannon road, passing through Dromad village on the way. When you have travelled for 7.0 miles, you will see the Mohill road to your right with a sign for Lough McHugh. Take the right turn, and go along this road for 2.6 miles where you will see a road to your left at the bad turn. Go up this road for 0.7 of a mile, and turn left up a narrow lane. When you have travelled for 0.3 of a mile, you will meet a second house on your left with a silver gate on the right. Go through this gate *(remember to close the gate)* and drive on down through the wood to the lakeshore. There is plenty of parking space in this area. On the small island there is a chestnut tree growing – how it got there is a mystery to me.

NOTE:

> The Fishery Board released 150 tench into McHugh during June of 2004. Let's hope they settle in well and increase in numbers and size over the coming years.

Lough Errill (5)

Our next visit brings us to Lough Errill. A shallow lake that offers up only limited shore fishing. Errill is quite a large lake and a rubber dinghy would be

the ideal way to explore it. This fishery is noted for its tench fishing with roach, rudd, hybrids, perch and pike also present. However, I must

This wooden stand on Lough Errill is ideal for the disabled angler. A tough fishery to have success on, however, the rewards can be some fabulous tench fishing.

warn you Errill, like a lot of the lakes in this area, can be a hard fishery. An English angler who lives locally, told me of a friend of his who pre-baited the lake with sweetcorn for three consecutive days, he fished for the next two days, starting at the crack of dawn, and never got a bite from a tench. A few days later, another visiting angler had a great tench session with fourteen fish – just goes to show how unpredictable those wild Irish fish can be.

Verdict
There is a lovely wooden platform, as can be seen in the photo on page 26, built out to Errill lake. However, it is a pity the Fishery Board did not extend it further out onto the lake past the weed growth that is very prevalent during the summer months. There is a wooden stile at the left of the parking area that brings you into a field where there is a small amount of shore fishing. If you are willing to walk along this shoreline for around 250 metres, you will come to more wooden stands. This area is best for shore fishing – it was along this shore that Brian Bohan caught those nice plump tench – photo on page 80. Errill can be a very weedy fishery particularly late in the season. There is no proper place to launch a boat, however after all that, Errill is still worth a visit.

How to get there
Approaching from the Longford road, you drive straight on past the bridge at Roosky, and carry on out the N4 Carrick-on-Shannon road, passing through Dromad village on the way. When you have travelled 7.0 miles, you will see the Mohill road to your right with a sign for Lough McHugh. Go along this road for 2.4 miles. You will see Lough Errill down a lane to your right. Best of Luck.

Lough Cloonfinnan (6)

This is a first class coarse fishery. However, Cloonfinnan has no wooden stands and shore fishing is very limited. Once again, a boat would be the ideal way to get to the best spot. Cloonfinnan is a favourite with swans and other wildfowl, who are attracted by its lush weed growth. This fishery is noted for its big bream and tench as well as its superb pike fishing.

Verdict
Will the Fishery Board please build a few wooden platforms on this delightful fishery? I have fished Cloonfinnan on a number of occasions from my boat,

Adventurer, and I had some first class bream, tench and pike fishing. The lake is very weedy in places. Cloonfinnan is a shallow lake with a maximum depth of only five feet. Paddy and I are planning a return visit to this fishery some time in late winter when weed growth has died down. We hope to encounter one of the huge pike that are reported to be lurking in Cloonfinnan. the photo on the back cover is of local angler Brian Bohan with a fabulous catch of twenty-eight tench caught on Lough Cloonfinnan. Lough Cloonfinnan is the classic wild Irish fishery.

How to get there

Approaching from the Longford road, you head straight past Roosky bridge and keep going along the N4 Carrick-on-Shannon road passing through Dromad village on the way, for exactly 7.0 miles. At this point you will meet a road to your right with a sign for Lough McHugh. Turn up this road and go along for 1.9 miles, where you will meet a small road to your right. Go down this road for 1.2 miles and you will find you can park at the entrance to the lake on your right – there is shore fishing at this point, also a boat-launching area. For more shore fishing keep up to your right for about 100 metres. Along this stretch of shoreline the lake averages about four feet in depth. Tight Lines.

Exploring the catch — Brian Bohan with that fabulous bag of wild Irish tench on the shore of Lough Cloonfinnan.

Bog Lough (7)

When I first visited Bog Lough I was enchanted by the peace and quiet and the dark mysterious location. From reports I have received from two visiting British anglers it looks like Bog Lough is a real bream and tench hot spot, however, shore fishing is limited. I have fished Bog Lough on only one occasion from a rubber dinghy. I was in pursuit of its pike, and gathering information on the various depths. On this occasion, I had no luck with its pike population, however the fish finder showed up some large fish in Bog Lough.

Verdict

Bog Lough is about 100 metres from the road. When you get down to the lake – go along the barbed wire fence to your left until you come to a wood, go into the wood and keep over to your right, you will meet an oak tree growing at the edge of the lake. There's plenty of shore fishing at this point, into four to six feet of water. At its deepest which is near the centre, and up to the right, the lake goes down to between eight to ten feet. I fed Bog Lough for three consecutive days during June 2004, prior to a visit by two British anglers, Dave Towel and Stuart Sprigings. They fished it on the fourth day from 9.30am to 6.00pm and could only manage two small rudd. Brian Bohan pre-baited a swim for a few days prior to a visit in July 2004. Brian fished the lake from late evening to the following morning, he could only manage some rudd, hybrids, eels, small bream with one large one to 7lb. Bog Lough is a rich fishery with lots of feeding for its

fish life, it might take a bit more perseverance on the part of the angler to really bag up on this lake. Woods surround Bog Lough as you can see in the photo on left.

Stuart Springing and Dave Towel from Notts in England, setting up on the shore of the Bog Lough, No. 7 in the Ten Stepping Stones.

How to get there

Approaching the Roosky Bridge from the Longford road, you head straight out the N4 Carrick-on-Shannon road for 3.5 miles, passing through Dromad village on the way. There is a sharp turn on the right at this point, go down this narrow rough road and under a railway bridge for 0.9 of a mile. Park at the gate on your left – the lake is down at the end of the field. Best of luck.

Cloonturk Lough (8)

This small reedy fishery is definitely for the exploring angler. I don't know any way other than with a rubber dinghy to get fishing on Cloonturk. When I first visited this lake in the summer of 2002, the water level was quite high as can be seen in the photo. At the time, I thought this could be a real gem of a fishery. However, on another visit in the summer of 2003, this time from the narrow road that leads down to Bog Lough, I found the lake very low and not a fishing prospect. On this occasion I was filming Cloonturk for my new video which will accompany this book.

Verdict

The Eslin River runs alongside Cloonturk. On my first visit during that very wet summer of 2002, the river had overflowed into the lake, giving it the appearance of a nice coarse fishery, pictured below. However, when the river runs low the lake dries up into small ponds. Cloonturk is a bit of a mystery – I have a feeling this lake is rarely fished. Who knows? It could be a first class coarse fishery, waiting for the exploring angler to bravely go where no

A view out to Lough Cloonturk in high water levels. The level of this wild fishery depends on the height the river Eslin is running – this river is in the foreground of the photo.

angler has gone before. About two miles from Cloonturk the Eslin River enters the Shannon near Roosky, so it's possible in high floods, that various fish species could travel up to Cloonturk from the Shannon. Upstream the Eslin River runs out of Cloonboniagh Lough, so fish could easily make the short journey down to Cloonturk.

How to get there

Approaching the bridge at Roosky from the Longford road, you head straight on out the N4 Carrick-on-Shannon road for 1.8 miles. Take the right turn in Dromad village and go out the Mohill road for 1.3 miles where you will meet a gate on your left. Park here; there is a little blue painted house on the opposite side of the road. Go through the gate and you will have to walk nearly 450 metres up a long field, remember you are on private property at this point, so permission from the farmer at the house would be advisable. At the top of the field, you will meet a hedge dividing you from the river Eslin and Lough Cloonturk as you can see in the photo on page 30. A rubber dinghy would be the best option for fishing this lake. There is another way into Cloonturk on the right of the narrow road that leads to Bog Lough. You travel up this road, going under the railway bridge for 0.5 of a mile, where you will meet a gate on your right. Park here, you might just be able to see the lake down through the fields. Another possibility would be to navigate by boat up the Eslin River from the Shannon. If you make the journey – best of luck! You certainly deserve it.

Cloonboniagh Lough (9)

This is a delightful fishery situated along the Dromad/Mohill road. There is extensive shore fishing along the roadside.

This visiting angler from Northampton in England, pictured relaxing along the shore of Cloonboniagh.

Cloonboniagh is of a peaty nature. It has all the coarse fish species – I have taken some nice bream and tench as well as pike to 14lb from this delightful lake. There is also good rudd, roach, hybrid and perch fishing. I have heard reports of large pike present in this fishery.

Verdict

A must for the visiting angler. Cloonboniagh or as it is often called locally Clonboney offers up easy access as well as plenty of easy shore fishing. There is ample parking space beside the lake. A rubber dinghy would be the ideal way to cover the lake – boat launch would be difficult as the gate into the lake is locked.

How to get there

From the bridge at Roosky, head straight out the N4 Carrick-on-Shannon road for 1.8 miles and then turn right in Dromad village and head on out the Mohill road for 2.1 miles. You will see the parking space on your left. There are steps down to the lake at this point. When you go down the steps, keep over to your left where you will find a wooden stand. Photo of visiting angler from Northamptonshire in England on previous page.

Gubagraffy and Roosky Loughs (10– 11)

As hard as I tried, I honestly could not find any trace of these two lakes. It was during the month of June 2003 when I visited for the purposes of this book. I believe they are what we call in Ireland "turloughs". These flood in winter and dry up again in summer – also they could have been drained for turf cutting purposes.

Both lakes were situated off the Mohill road. When you turn right in Dromad village, keep going to the second right turn at 0.65 of a mile. Gubagraffy was 1.2 miles on the right down this boggy road, while Roosky Lough was in on the left near the end of the road, another 0.85 of a mile.

Drumard Lough (12)

This is a small interesting little fishery, which is rarely fished. I have heard local reports of good pike, roach and rudd fishing. I have not fished Drumard and can only give information on a visit during June of 2003 for the purposes of this book. The lake was very low and impossible to fish from the shore, maybe in high water levels you will get fishing from the shore. The best bet would be from a rubber dinghy, however you will have a long journey to bring it to the lake.

Verdict

Drumard needs a little negotiating to get to as it lies about 500 metres down through the fields. This lake is definitely for the exploring angler who will need to carry very little fishing gear. Who knows? Drumard could well be a fabulous little coarse fishery. If you ever fish it, I hope you bag up like never before. Believe me you will have earned it.

How to get there

Slightly new directions. From the bridge in Roosky you head straight out the N4 Carrick-on-Shannon road for just 0.1 of a mile. Take the right turn here just past Shannon Key West Hotel and head up this road for 1.9 miles, passing over the railway line on the way. Take a right turn here and travel along this road for a further 1.9 miles, where you take a left turn at Fox's pub. Go along this road for 2.1 miles with Lough Rinn on your right, you will see a gate in to your left. Park on the far side of the road, go in through the gate and follow the pathway down to the end of the first field. Go right here into the next field, keep over to the left

where you will have to go through a gap in the hedge. The lake is down at end of the next field. Best of luck – you are going to need it!

This small fishery is rarely fished. A lake for the exploring angler. Lough Drumard could well be a nice coarse fishery.

Lough Rinn (13)

We are now visiting the largest lake in Area 3. Rinn Lough is long and narrow. On its east bank stands Lough Rinn House and Gardens – a magnificent period residence which as I write these notes is closed to the public for renovation work. When it reopens, do pay it a visit. Within the grounds of the estate, there is extensive shore fishing into four to six feet of water. The area at the back of the gardens is often the most productive, however you can have good sport along any part of this shoreline, which is mainly weed-free.

Verdict

An enchanting lake; I have spent many hours of delightful fishing on Lough Rinn. The bream and tench fishing can be first class, especially if the swim has been previously ground baited. Roach-rudd hybrids, perch and eels are also present. Rinn also holds big pike. My heaviest to date weighed in at 18lbs 2ozs. Paddy's was slightly heavier at 20lbs 6ozs. Some friends of mine have had pike well over the 20lb mark. The upper half of the lake is quite shallow, only going to between three to six feet in depth. As you head down the lake below Rinn House, it gets much deeper, going down to twenty-four feet. This part of the lake often fishes best for those big pike. There are also reports of large brown trout present in this delightful fishery.

How to get there

Approaching the Roosky bridge from the Longford road, you go straight on out

the N4 Carrick-on-Shannon road for just 0.1 of a mile and take the right turn here just past Shannon Key West Hotel. Keep along

That's me with my trusty Suzuki Jeep, ready to unload my boat *Adventurer* onto Rinn Lough. Since acquiring the Jeep, I am now able to bring my boat to lakes that were previously out of bounds.

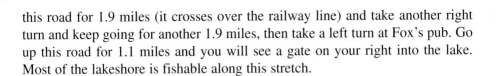

this road for 1.9 miles (it crosses over the railway line) and take another right turn and keep going for another 1.9 miles, then take a left turn at Fox's pub. Go up this road for 1.1 miles and you will see a gate on your right into the lake. Most of the lakeshore is fishable along this stretch.

The next place to fish from the shore is 1.3 miles further on, where there is an entry into the wood on your right. If you go in here, keep to your left, you will find wooden stands onto the lake – fishing here is into four to six feet of water. For the next fishable area, you travel on for a further 0.75 of a mile and you come to an amenity area where there is plenty of parking space as well as a boat launching area. If you keep left and go behind the caravan park, this area often proves to be a tench hot spot, here you will be fishing into three to five feet of water. To find two wooden stands, as you approach the concrete jetty, you drive up the small road to your right, for about sixty to seventy metres, when you come to the left turn park here – you will see a pass into the wood on your left. You must walk along this pass for about 256 metres where the first stand is in on your left. The second wooden stand is 110 metres further on into the left. I have found the first stand offers up more clear water to fish into. You will be fishing into three to five feet of water from both stands. The final place for shore fishing is in the grounds of Lough Rinn House. To get there you travel on from the amenity area for 0.25 of a mile and take a right turn, go along this road for another 0.25 of a mile and then turn right. The entrance to Lough Rinn House is 0.45 of a mile further on to your right. The best shore fishing lies behind the walled gardens, where you will be fishing into four to six feet. If you are a keen gardener, do pay a visit to the gardens that lie within the estate. Best of luck.

A nice hybrid for Brian Bohan on the shore of Lough Rinn. This part of the lake lies behind Rinn House. On this day in July 2004, Brian had a fabulous days fishing to mainly roach and hybrids.

Creenagh Lake (14)

We have now journeyed over to a nice sized lake – Creenagh is a dark deep mysterious fishery. Sometimes you can have first class bream and tench fishing; other times the lake can prove very frustrating with long spells of fruitless fishing. Why this should be I honestly do not know. There are also plenty of rudd-roach hybrids, as well as large perch and pike in Lough Creenagh.

Verdict
Well worth a visit, Creenagh has been well catered for by the Fishery Board with a total of four wooden platforms to fish from. Be careful, some of them are getting on in age and not as sturdy as they once were. You can ledger here for those difficult bream and tench, or try your hand at capturing one of its large pike. Best of luck.

How to get there
Approaching the Roosky Bridge from the Longford road, you head straight on out the N4 Carrick-on-Shannon road for just 0.1 of a mile and take a turn to your right, just past the Shannon Key West Hotel. You drive along this road for 1.9 miles crossing over the railway line on your way. Take a right turn here and head straight on for another 1.9 miles. Here you take a left turn at Fox's pub and head along this road for 4.2 miles. You will pass Lough Rinn on your right. Take the right turn here and go on up this road for 0.8 of a mile. You will now see Creenagh Lake on your left. Park at the lay-by on your right. There are two ways into the lake – one is at the gate beside a small building, or

These two British anglers, Steve Cooper on left and Terry Gibbons from Shropshire pictured camping out on the shore of Creenagh Lake.

further up the road on your left, where there is a wooden stile into a wood that brings you to the lake. Fishing from the platforms is into five to seven feet of water. Best of luck. Remember "patience is a virtue" – you might just need some on this fishery. Photo of visiting angler Ian Young with some nice tench from Creenagh on page 72.

NOTE:

> During late June of 2004, Brian Bohan after ground baiting the swim for three previous days, fished Creenagh from the wooden stand. After an all night session, Brian never caught a fish. In the early morning, he spotted large bream rolling about twenty metres beyond his hook bait, but they did not venture into his swim. In September 2004, on a return visit to Creenagh, Ian Young had a great day's fishing to mainly large roach and hybrids.

Lough Sallagh – first (15)

As hard as I tried, I could not find Sallagh Lake. Maybe it dries up during the summer months or maybe I did not try hard enough! This lake should be just up from Lough Errew on the Cloone river. I can say nothing more about Lough Sallagh except if you do manage to discover it, please let me know!

Lough Errew (16)

This seems to be a fascinating looking Lough. I have never fished Errew but hope to pay it a visit with my rubber dinghy. Errew is joined to Lough Rinn by a short stretch of the Rinn River.

Verdict

Oh! How I tried to find shore fishing on this beautiful lake – but without success. I have a feeling the Fishery Board must have built a wooden stand onto Lough Errew, however I couldn't locate it. A rubber dinghy seems to be the best alternative. It could be launched onto the lake via the Rinn River. There is one other possibility from the far shore where there are the ruins of an old estate, however it would mean a long walk down through some rough land. If you manage to fish Lough Errew I have a feeling you could be in for a great day's fishing. Best of luck.

How to get there

I am going to give two directions for you to check out, if you are intent on fishing this mysterious Lough. The first is to the Rinn River near Lough Rinn House. Once again approaching the Roosky bridge from the Longford road, you go straight on out the N4 Carrick-on-Shannon road for just 0.1 of a mile. Take the right turn here just past the Shannon Key West Hotel and head up this road for 1.9 miles crossing the railway line on the way. Take a right turn at this stage and carry on for another 1.9 miles, take the left turn here at Fox's pub and keep going for 3.4 miles and then take the right turn in towards Lough Rinn House. Go along for 0.25 of a mile and then take another right turn. Keep along this road for 0.75 of a mile until you meet the bridge over the river. Errew is in to your left. On a visit during the summer of 2003, when I was doing some videoing, I met up with some French anglers who were about to travel the short journey to Errew via the small river – they were using two rubber dinghies and in pursuit of pike.

The second possibility for shore fishing is on the far shore. Go back to the directions to Creenagh Lake. At Creenagh, you travel further on up this road for 2.5 miles and you will see a gate on your right. From this point you can see the lake a long way in the distance. There is a laneway down to the ruins of an old house. When you get to the house you will have a long journey to walk to get to the lake. Best of luck.

NOTE:

> With the new development that is going on at Rinn House I heard reports that the land adjacent to Lough Errew is going to be part of a new golf course – if this is the case, then there could well be plenty of shore fishing on Errew in the future.

Clooncoe or Drumbad Lough (17)

We are now visiting a noted tench fishery, Clooncoe Lough or as it is known locally, Drumbad which also offers up good bream, perch, pike, roach, rudd and hybrid fishing. This is a lovely tranquil lake that is surrounded by a thick forest of conifers and deciduous trees – Clooncoe is rarely fished. It is a gem of a lake for the exploring angler.

Verdict

If you are into tench fishing Drumbad could be just the lake for you. I have heard reports of tench between 8lb and 9lb being taken regularly on this fishery. Drumbad also offers up some of the best rudd fishing in the Irish Midlands, as well as plenty of large pike. If you are in these parts I would highly recommend a visit to Drumbad. There is plenty of shore fishing – in places you might have to negotiate high reeds.

Brian Bohan is pictured on page 40 with two nice plump wild Irish tench on the shore of Drumbad. After I took this photo, Brian fished on for another couple of hours, and had nine more tench – the heaviest weighing in at 7.5lbs. He also had up on 40lbs of mainly rudd. The successful method was ledgering at thirty to forty metres, using three or four red maggots as bait.

How to get there

At Roosky bridge go straight on out the N4 Carrick-on-Shannon road for just 0.1 of

a mile, turn right here just past the Shannon Key West Hotel and continue on this road for a further 1.9 miles and take a right turn. Keep on this road for a further 1.9 miles until you reach Fox's pub

A dark mysterious fishery, Lough Drumbad pictured looking up from the rocky shore.

on your left. This time you go straight on for 0.9 of a mile, take second left turn with large two storey stone house on the opposite side of road. Go along this road for a further 1.55 miles where you will see a small road in to your left with a fishing sign saying 'Lough Drumbad'. Go on down this road for 0.4 of a mile keeping right. Go through the first gate for parking. The lake is through the next gate on your left. Head down to the lake where you will see shore fishing among the reeds. If you keep up to your left and cross the wooden stile you will find easier shore fishing. You can continue over the wooden stiles along this shore, where you will meet plenty more shore fishing. When you meet the lake, you can keep right and go through the wood where you can fish among large rocks.

Tight Lines.

LOUGH DRUMBAD

Brian Bohan with two nice tench from this fabulous tench fishery.

Drumshanbo Lough (18)
— The 1st Stepping-Stone —

Drumshanbo lake – what mysteries does it hold? I have been wondering about this since I first noticed it while on a trout fishing trip with an angling friend, Joe Carr, to the Cloone River over thirty years ago. I could see the lake on the left side of the Cloone road lying peacefully below an upland bog. I have not fished Drumshanbo and can only give advice based on a visit made for the purposes of this book.

Verdict
Drumshanbo is rarely fished and it is my belief that it could be a fabulous bream fishery. This is a hunch on my part but with Sallagh Lough just over the far side of the Cloone road, the evidence points in this direction. The lake lies a long way down through the fields. There is some shore fishing if you negotiate the weeds. A lake for the exploring angler, who could be rewarded with some excellent sport, that could well include some 20lb+ pike. If you do fish Drumshanbo let me know how you got on.

How to get there
I am now giving new directions, this time from Drumlish crossroads. Approaching from the Longford road you go straight on at the crossroads in Drumlish, heading out the Arvagh road for 0.4 of a mile and turn left out the Cloone road. Go along this road for 1.2 miles keeping left at the dangerous junction, keep going past the junction for 2.3 miles until you see a left turn, go down this road for 0.2 of a mile. Park at the gate on the left, you will see the lake down two fields on your right.

Keeldra Lake (19)

I have fished Keeldra on several occasions, both from a boat and from the shore. The quarry was always pike. I must say I enjoyed my visits and have had several pike in the double figures. The heaviest weighed in at around 16lb. I did not keep a diary, but from memory, I also caught quite a few over the 10lb mark. Paddy also loves to visit Keeldra. I have been told that Keeldra holds mainly pike and perch – there is very little in the way of other coarse fish in the lake.

Verdict

The lake is well worth a visit for its ease of fishing and quiet location. Keeldra is a clear, shallow lake with a stony bottom. On a recent visit in March of 2003, I noticed the water in the lake was a green colour at the amenity area, however I had a good day's pike fishing, catching a total of eight pike. The heaviest weighed in at around 9lb. The successful baits were my red and white plug and a dead smelt trolled behind my small dingy *Adventurer*. Keeldra is between twelve and fourteen feet at its deepest point, which is down the middle of the lake. Along the shore the lake falls of to a depth of eight to ten feet. If you're boat fishing keep up to the left of the amenity area, until you meet the end of the lake, and keep over to the right – I have found this area a pike hot spot. Over to the right, off the amenity area and out from the small boathouse is another good area for pike. I have taken some decent perch close to the 2lb mark while trolling for pike on Keeldra. Tight Lines.

How to get there

Approaching the crossroads in Drumlish from the Longford road, you head straight out the Arvagh road for 0.4 of a mile until you meet the Cloone road on your left. Take this turn and keep along this road for 1.2 miles and then take the left turn at the dangerous junction. Keep going for a further 5.6 miles. Go down the road on the right for 0.3 of a mile where there is a gate into your right. This entry allows you extensive shore fishing on this side of the lake. Keep to your left at the small boat house, where there's often good shore fishing. Next go further on for another 0.2 of a mile until you meet an amenity area at the side of the lake, there is plenty of shore fishing in this area as well as boat launching facilities. There is also shore fishing to be had if you travel 0.4 of a mile further on the road until you meet a large tree on your right on the hill – park here and go down the fields to the lake. There is some excellent shore fishing to be had here from a rocky shoreline. Best of luck.

NOTE:

During June of 2003, I revisited Lough Keeldra to do some videoing – on this occasion the lake was crystal clear. I don't know what happened to the green colour, I presume it was some sort of an algae that cleared up. There was also a man swimming in the lake.

In the middle of June 2004 the Fishery Board released close on 100 large tench into Keeldra. As far as I know this is the first time tench have been in this lake. Let's hope they establish themselves and offer up good fishing in the future.

Sallagh Lake – second (20)
— The 2nd Stepping Stone —

The second of the Ten Stepping Stones, Lough Sallagh is a noted bream, rudd and pike fishery. It is a favourite with Paddy and me – we have had regular catches of bream up around the 100lb mark. In recent years there has been a lot of reclamation work done along the shore of the lake – where a nice amenity area has been developed, as well as plenty of parking space. Sallagh has a long shoreline with easy access for the angler to fish from. The average depth of Lough Sallagh is only four feet it can also be very weedy in parts particularly around the middle.

Ready for action – this visiting British angler on the shore of Lough Sallagh. This is a top class coarse fishery.

Paddy's Discovery

It was during a wildfowling trip in the late 1960s when Paddy first discovered the bream potential of Lough Sallagh. A few friends invited him for an evening's duck shooting on Sallagh Lake over near Drumlish. Paddy readily accepted and was looking forward to shooting a few ducks for the dinner.

It was early September, after a long hot and dry summer, the weather had turned very wet causing widespread flooding. When Paddy arrived at the lake the water level was well up onto the fields near the road side. On closer inspection he also noticed a lot of water disturbance was happening on the flooded pastureland along the lakeshore. This called for further investigation on Paddy's part. He waded out near to where the disturbance was happening and discovered it was being caused by large shoals of bream, which were feasting on worms and snails that were trapped when the grassland flooded.

The next day Paddy called to see me, he was excited about this mysterious lake over near Drumlish where the bream shoals were huge. Paddy explained what he discovered while out shooting and was mad keen to head over for an evening's fishing. I was quite excited myself and as it was getting near the end of the season, we decided we had better head over as soon as possible.

It was Saturday afternoon before I could go. Paddy offered to collect the bait; small red brandling worms, which were in plentiful supply in the dung heaps beside the college cowsheds. Paddy reckoned nature had done the ground baiting for us when the water flooded the pastureland.

It was around 6.00pm, when we arrived at Sallagh Lake. There was only a slight wind and I remember remarking how peaceful and calm the lake was looking, we tackled up and put our keep-net out in anticipation of a good evenings fishing. We baited up with the red worms and decided to fish on the bottom forty metres out in a depth of about three feet of water. At the time, we used silver paper taken from cigarette packets as our bite indicator. It was now a case of waiting for the shoals of bream Paddy was talking about to make their way out of their deep water hideout and venture into our swim.

After about an hour of waiting, there was still no sign of the bream. Suspicion began to enter my thoughts. I asked Paddy was he sure we were at the right lake. "Bernie, patience is not your strong point! Of course this is the right lake,"

replied Paddy. Another half hour passed without any movement. The lake was now flat calm. I turned to Paddy: "Maybe they have decided to feed on the far shore". "No Bernie, that shoreline is much higher and surrounded by reeds. It is this shoreline they will be heading for. They have probably gorged themselves for the past few evenings on nature's bounty, and are now a bit slower to make their way over" – with that a wide grin appeared on Paddy's face. "Bernie look up along the shoreline about sixty yards to your right, I think I saw a disturbance on the surface. Look! I was right – they are on the move!" Paddy was right. The bream were moving onto the flooded pastureland. "Will we move up to where they are?" I asked. "No Bernie they will make their way down this far. When they do, I will do a bit of ground baiting with this tin of worms." Paddy had brought a biscuit tin full of worms to entice and keep the bream in our swim.

Wee Celebration

The bream were slow, very slow to make their way along the shoreline. Paddy decided to take some action. He moved up with a handful of worms and tossed them out into the lake, when the bream moved down to feed, Paddy encouraged them with another handful of goodies. Eventually they entered our swim. "Now Bernie get ready for some hectic sport!" said Paddy.

Paddy was right; my silver paper started to move. It was a nice sized bream of about 5lbs. "Good start" remarked Paddy. Inside the next hour myself and Paddy were doing an Irish jig at the side of the lake, we were into a magnificent spell. Our net was nearly full. In fact, it was so full of bream we decided to release them back into the lake. We continued fishing, releasing each bream as we caught them – how many and how much they weighed, I wouldn't know. But it was the best bream fishing session we ever had.

We fished on till nightfall. I remember well when we decided to stop for the day. Paddy's satisfaction was evident. "Well Bernie! What did you think of that fishing session?"
"Paddy I will never forget it. We will have to make our way back for another evening's fishing before the season ends," I replied.
"Do you think it calls for a wee celebration?" asked Paddy.
The hint was easily entertained as I felt a sense of achievement and satisfaction in what was our best ever bream session, and still remains so to this day.

O'Reillys pub in Drumlish was the stop off. There is one thing about North Longford people – they are fiercely proud of their rich fishing environment and love to hear it praised by visiting anglers. We had our waders on.

"How did your day's fishing go?" was the first question thrown at us in the pub. Paddy knew how to relax the locals.

"Fabulous area for fishing. Annagh lake is packed full of bream, we were catching them every few minutes". Paddy's secrets are Paddy's secrets.

There is something peaceful and relaxed about fishermen. Strangers feel comfortable in their company. In fact rural people can relate quite easily to anglers. We were in good company. Drumlish can be a great village for the craic.

How to get there

Approaching from the Longford road, you go straight out the Arvagh road, at the crossroads in Drumlish for 0.4 of a mile. From there, you take a left turn down the Cloone road for 1.2 miles. Then you keep right at the dangerous junction (remember to give right of way). Go up this road for 1.55 miles, take the left turn at the sign for Sallagh lake. Go along this narrow road for 0.8 of a mile to where the extensive shoreline meets the road. You can fish here at the amenity area – if you go on for another 0.3 of a mile you will come to a clearing to your left at the edge of the lake – you can launch a boat here or fish along the weed-free shoreline. Some year's weed growth can affect different parts of the shoreline. Previous heavy ground baiting can be a big help in getting the bream into your swim, and do not forget, last thing at night, first thing in the morning. Sallagh also offers up top class pike fishing, however trolling on the lake is very difficult because of all the weeds. I have found this upper part of the lake to be the most weed-free area. Tight Lines.

NOTE:

In the middle of June 2004, the Fishery Board released 200 tench into Sallagh. As far as I know these are the first tench in Sallagh, which should be an ideal lake for them – most of the bed of Sallagh Lake is covered in a fine black mud, which should suit tench. Sallagh is an extremely rich fishery – I have often checked the green weed for aquatic life. I have found the weed to be teeming with mainly nymphs, shrimps, snails and masses of freshwater louses.

Fearglass Lough (21)
– The 3rd Stepping Stone —

This time we are making the short journey from Sallagh to Fearglass Lough – the third lake in the Ten Stepping Stones. A lovely scenic coarse fishery with good bream fishing, Fearglass also holds rudd, roach, hybrids as well as big pike and perch. I have fished it on a few occasions the bream catches were not nearly as good as on Sallagh Lake. However, they were always over the 50lbs mark, with fish ranging between 3lbs and 6lbs.

Verdict
This is another fishery that is well worth a visit. There is no problem with shore fishing – in fact you can fish the lake around most of its shoreline. However, there is quite a long walk down to the lake, which is around 500 metres through some rough land. Fearglass is a very picturesque lake in a wild terrain and a must for the short list.

How to get there
Approaching from the Longford road you go straight out the Arvagh road, at the crossroads in Drumlish for 0.4 of a mile and then you take the left turn out the Cloone road. Go on along this road for a further 1.2 miles and then turn right, at the dangerous junction (remember to give right of way). Keep along this road for another 2.6 miles until you meet a crossroads (the 98 Pub is on your right). Turn left here, the gate into the lake is 0.6 of a mile down this road on your left. At its deepest point, which is out in the centre of the lake, Fearglass goes down to a depth of twenty-five feet. From the shore you will be fishing into around four to eight feet of water. Up to the right where the river leaves the lake and

flows down to Clooncose, often proves the most productive. Best of Luck.

This picturesque fishery lies a long way down the fields. Fearglass offers up loads of easy shore fishing to bream, roach, rudd, pike and perch.

Clooncose Lake (22)
— The 4th Stepping Stone —

Just below Fearglass on the opposite side of the road lies Clooncose Lake. This is a very inaccessible fishery. I have never fished this lake. On a visit, for the purposes of this book, I could find no area for shore fishing. The edge of the lake was overgrown with high reeds and very soft under foot. A rubber dinghy would be ideal for this fishery, as you would only have a short journey to carry it.

Verdict

This would be an ideal lake for the Fishery Board to build some wooden platforms on – this would enable the visiting angler to uncover its mysteries. As hard as I tried I could find no one with information about Clooncose. It seems it is rarely fished, or maybe the locals are keeping the secrets of this wild fishery to themselves. When I get the chance, maybe sometime during 2004, I think myself and Paddy will be heading off with our rubber dingy *Explorer*, to find out for ourselves what lies beneath the surface of Clooncose.

How to get there

Follow the directions to Fearglass Lough – from the gate at Fearglass, you head down the road and over the small river, you will see the sign for the lake on your right. Keep going past this sign until you see a gate on your right, that brings you into Clooncose. If you manage to fish it before me please let me know how you got on. PS — it's almost a year since I visited this mysterious fishery, and I am still wondering, why no one seems to know anything about it?

Potentially a cracker of a fishery. The problem with Clooncose is finding shore fishing.

NOTE:

During July of 2004, I paid a visit to Tooman Angling Shop in Carrick-on-Shannon. Tony showed me a photo of two British anglers with a catch of nearly 100lb of mainly bream taken from Clooncose. Photo on page 48. This photo was taken back in 1997. As can be seen in the photo, they found a good swim. I am not sure where this swim is – if you are in Tony's shop he might be able to give you better information on this fishery.

Lough Nabelwy (23)
– The 5th Stepping Stone –

The next lake on our journey is Lough Nabelwy. A nice, easily fished water with plenty of shore fishing. This fishery is also ideal for launching a boat as it comes to within a few metres of the roadway. Nabelwy is quite shallow, only reaching a depth of between six and seven feet in the middle – along the shore you will find yourself fishing into three to five feet of water.

Verdict
I have fished Lough Nabelwy on only one occasion from my boat *Adventurer*. I was in pursuit of pike and had a good day's fishing with a total of six fish, the heaviest weighing in at 12lbs. The successful baits were dead smelt and roach trolled behind the boat. This is a lovely little fishery that nestles down in a valley. There are local reports of good bream fishing. The top of the lake where the small river runs in from Clooncose, is heavily overgrown with lily pads. Once again I have that fisherman's feeling, that this could be a fabulous tench fishery. Put the fifth of the Ten Stepping Stones, Lough Nabelwy, on your short list.

How to get there
Go straight on out the Arvagh road from the crossroads in Drumlish for 0.4 of a mile. Turn down Cloone road on your left, go along this road for another 1.2 miles and then take the right turn at the dangerous junction (remember to give right of way). Keep along this road for 2.6 miles where you meet a crossroads with pub on your right. Take a slight left here, you must now cross the road, and then go straight on for 0.7 of a mile and take the road into your left. Go down this road with the graveyard on your left for 0.8 of a mile and you will find a parking place on your left. Tight Lines.

NOTE:

In the middle of June 2004, the Shannon Fishery Board released close on 100 tench into this delightful fishery.

Doogary Lough (24)
– The 6th Stepping Stone –

Another one of those wild fisheries, Doogary is a long, narrow straggling lake. From a conversation I had with a local landowner, it seems the lake is rarely fished. It holds stocks of rudd, bream, tench and pike. There are local reports of an angler losing a monster pike on the lake during the summer of 1999. On a visit during the summer of 2003, when I was filming for my new video, I found the side of the lake completely covered in lily pads, and impossible to fish from the shore. The best option would be a rubber dinghy.

Verdict
I have not fished Lough Doogary and can only go on what information I have been given. The lake seems fairly shallow. A river runs into Doogary from Lough Nabelwy and out again into Gortermone, so migration of fish in this area is quite easy, the farmer mentioned golden finned fish and shads in the lake, which I presume are rudd and bream. This is a very interesting fishery and well worth a visit.

How to get there
Approaching the crossroads in Drumlish from the Longford road, you head straight on out the Arvagh road for 0.4 of a mile. Take the left turn down Cloone road and go along this road for 1.2 miles and then take a right turn at the dangerous junction (remember to give right of way). Keep along this road for

2.6 miles where you will meet a cross-roads with a pub on your right. Take a slight left turn then cross the road and go straight on here

A nice peaceful scene of Lough Doogary. It was on this lake in June 2004 when Tony Egan had that fabulous bag of bream.

for 1.2 miles and take a left turn, go up this narrow road for 0.9 of a mile until you meet a narrow lane into your right. Go along this lane for 0.35 of a mile until you reach the end at four gates. The lake is down fields to your left. A rubber dinghy would be a huge advantage in exploring this lake. Best of luck and I hope you encounter that monster pike.

NOTE:

It was through a chance meeting with Peter Dillon who runs a pub and angling guesthouse in Ballinamuck, Co. Longford, that I found out some valuable information about Doogary. Peter told me about North Longford angler, Tony Egan, who had a fabulous bream session in early June 2004 on Doogary. Tony had just over 150lb of bream. Photo on front cover. This is the only information I have about this fishery, if you would like further information you could phone Tony on **086-3493044** or visit Peter Dillon's pub in Ballinamuck. As you enter the first field, you will see the lake down to your left, head straight across the field to the far hedge. At this hedge you will see a small stream that runs down to the lake. Seemingly you have to cross this stream to get to the best shore fishing.

Corglass Lough (25)

This is a small lake that lies two fields over from the end of a long lane. It is rarely – if ever – fished, mainly because there is no shore fishing with dense lily pads for about twenty metres onto the lake.

Verdict

Corglass is definitely for the exploring angler. I am sorry I have no information on this mystery lake, however a venture onto it via a rubber dinghy could well throw up some surprises. Like Doogary, I have a feeling there could well be some top class tench and bream fishing, for the angler who is brave enough to venture on to this fishery.

How to get there

Approaching from the Longford road, you head straight out the Arvagh road at the crossroads in Drumlish for 0.4 of a mile and take a left turn down Cloone road, keep along this road for 1.2 miles and keep right at the dangerous junction.

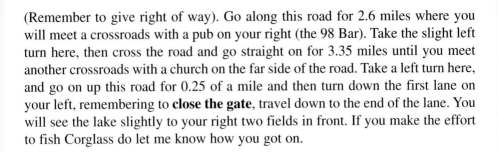

(Remember to give right of way). Go along this road for 2.6 miles where you will meet a crossroads with a pub on your right (the 98 Bar). Take the slight left turn here, then cross the road and go straight on for 3.35 miles until you meet another crossroads with a church on the far side of the road. Take a left turn here, and go on up this road for 0.25 of a mile and then turn down the first lane on your left, remembering to **close the gate**, travel down to the end of the lane. You will see the lake slightly to your right two fields in front. If you make the effort to fish Corglass do let me know how you got on.

Gortermone Lough (26)
— The 7th Stepping Stone —

The seventh of the Ten Stepping Stones, and the first of the three sister lakes. Gortermone Lough is a very accessible fishery with plenty of shore fishing. It is noted for its perch, pike, bream, roach and tench fishing. If you want an easy day's fishing, Gortermone is for you. In recent years, visiting British anglers have reported catching some nice tench on this lake.

Verdict
I have fished Gortermone from my boat *Adventurer*, on a number of occasions. I was trolling for pike using mainly small dead roach as bait, I have caught some nice pike, if my memory serves me right, the heaviest weighed in at around 16lb, and was taken on a trolled dead roach at the top end of the lake. This fishery

varies considerably in depth with the shallowest part in front of the small island at Lakeland Stores, where it is around two to five

After the photos, time to load up the catch. Tony Egan Jr and his friend John Hand are pictured on the shore of Lough Gortermone.

feet. As you approach the lake after coming down the steep hill, Gortermone is between eight and ten feet deep, if you keep left to where the trees are growing alongside the lake you will find depths of ten to eighteen feet. At its deepest, which is out in the middle, the lake goes down to twenty-seven feet.

How to get there

Approaching the Drumlish crossroads from the Longford road you head straight out the Arvagh road for 0.4 of a mile and turn left down the Cloone road. Keep along this road for 1.2 miles and then take a right turn at the dangerous junction, (remembering to give right of way). Keep along this road for 2.6 miles where you will meet a crossroads with a pub on your right (The 98 Bar). Take the slight left turn here, then cross road and go straight on here for 3.35 miles until you come to the crossroads facing the church, turn left here and drive along for 1.5 miles and you will see the lake on your left. You can park here and go on down the steep hill to where there is plenty of shore fishing. For more shore fishing and a boat launch area go further on the road for 0.1 of a mile and take the left turn, Lakeland Stores is just up the road on your left. There is a small lane into the lake at this point. The final place for shore fishing is just past Lakeland Stores, where you drive over the bridge and turn into your left, at this point you walk alongside the river. When you get near the lake keep right for plenty of comfortable shore fishing. Along this shore you will be fishing into around five to eight feet of water. Best of luck. Photo on previous page of local anglers Anthony Egan junior and friend John, with this fabulous catch of tench, bream, roach and hybrids, taken along shore just past Lakeland Stores.

NOTE:

Around 4.30 on the afternoon of Friday 30th of July 2004, I received a phone call from Anthony Egan Junior. Anthony and his friend John were on the shore of Gortermone Lough, they had a good day fishing and wanted to know if I would like to call over to take some photos and do some videoing.

I arrived at the lake at around 6.00pm to find the two lads fishing the shore up to the right pass Lakeland Stores. They had a great day fishing to mainly bream and tench, the successful bait was three small worms and three maggots on a size 12 hook. This was fished on the bottom with a feeder about forty yards out in six feet of water. The previous day they had heavily ground baited the swims.

While I was at the lake, I noticed the shallows were teaming with small fish fry. On further investigation thanks to the loan of Anthony's net I discovered a variety of different coarse fish species. The spring of 2004 must have been ideal for spawning fish, and as Gortermone is linked via a river to most of the lakes in this area, anglers can look forward to bumper fishing in this part of the Irish Midlands.

Tully Lough (27)
— The 8th stepping stone —

The second of the three sister lakes, Tully is noted for its good bream, tench, hybrid, perch and pike fishing. This lake is a delight to fish with lots of shore fishing. It is over twenty-five years since I first visited Tully and have been in love with it ever since. Paddy and I have had 50lb plus catches from Tully as well as several pike close to the 20lb mark.

Verdict
I would recommend Tully for a visit, it is a favourite with Paddy who never refuses an invitation to fish Tully, put this lake on your agenda when visiting these parts. You should not be disappointed, especially if you had the chance to get in plenty of ground bait prior to your fishing visit. Tully is quite a deep fishery averaging between twenty-seven and thirty feet out in the middle. When you meet the lake at the end of the road, along this shore you will be fishing into depths of eight to ten feet. If you keep going on your left to as far as where the whin bushes are growing, roughly about 250 metres, you will be fishing into depths of sixteen to twenty feet. Tight Lines.

I took this photo of Tully Lough near to where the small river runs down to Beaghmore Lake. You can see my boat *Adventurer* in the very shallow water at this point of Tully.

How to get there

Approaching from the Longford road, you travel straight on from the crossroads in Drumlish heading out the Arvagh road for 0.4 of a mile. Take the left turn here out the Cloone road, continue along this road for 1.2 miles and keep right again at the dangerous junction, (remembering to give right of way). Stay on this road for another 2.6 miles where you will meet a crossroads with a pub on your right (the 98 Bar). Take a slight left turn here, then cross the road and go straight on for 3.35 miles to the crossroads with the church facing you on the far side of the road. Take a left turn here and keep going for 1.6 miles and then take a left turn passing Lakeland Stores on your left for 0.7 of a mile where you take a right turn. Keep going along this road for 0.6 of a mile until you see a narrow road to your right. Go down this rough road that brings you to the shore of the lake remembering to **close the gate**. Tight Lines. Photo of Tully Lough on previous page.

Beaghmore Lake (28)
– The 9th Stepping Stone —

Next, we come to Beaghmore Lough, the last of the three sister lakes. At this point maybe I should explain why I call them the three sister lakes. Over the years, I have enjoyed many a happy day's pike fishing on these three fisheries. I usually start off on Lough Gortermone with my boat *Adventurer*, when I have satisfied myself on this fishery I head down the small river which brings me to Tully Lough. After fishing on Tully, I can journey down another short stretch of river, this time to Lough Beaghmore. A word of warning here, in very dry weather the small river between Tully and Beaghmore can become shallow at the point where it runs out of Tully. In these conditions, I pull my boat down the river until I find sufficient depth. For the visiting angler with a boat or rubber dinghy, who enjoys exploring fisheries the three sister lakes could offer up a great camping and fishing holiday.

Verdict

Getting back to Beaghmore, for the shore angler this fishery lies a long way down through the fields, and the minimum of equipment is advised. When you get to the lake, keep left for plenty of easy shore fishing. I have had some nice bream, rudd, roach and hybrid sessions on Beaghmore. This lake also offers up good pike fishing, my heaviest weighed in at 14lb and Paddy has taken a larger

fish of 21lb, and lost what he reckons was a fish near to the 30lb mark. There are the remains of old wooden stands on Beaghmore. I remember my first visit to this fishery almost thirty years ago, when the stands were in quite good shape, however the elements have taken their toll, and left them in a sorry state. Beaghmore could also produce some nice tench fishing. Photo of lake below.

How to get there
Approaching the Drumlish crossroads, from the Longford road you go straight on out the Arvagh road for 0.4 of a mile. Take the left turn here out the Cloone road, continue along this road for 1.2 miles and keep right at the dangerous junction, (remember to give right of way). Stay on this road for 2.6 miles until you reach a crossroads with a pub on your right (The 98 Bar). Take the slight left turn here, then cross the road and go straight on for 3.35 miles where you will meet a crossroads with a church facing you on the far side of the road. Take a left turn here and keep going for 1.6 miles then take another left turn, keep along this road for 0.7 of a mile passing Lakeland Stores on your left. Turn right here, and go up this road for 0.5 of a mile, where you will meet a house on your right. Beaghmore lies around 500 metres down behind this house. You can park between the laneway and the house. You must go down this grassy laneway for about twenty metres to the first gate. Keep going down the lane to the next gate. After this you will have to walk through some fields. When you are approaching the lake, keep over to your left and go through a gap in hedge into the next field. This is where you will find the best shore fishing. Tight Lines.

This is a rarely fished lake. As you can see from the photo there is plenty of shore fishing on Beaghmore. The old wooden stands are almost rotted away.

Annagh Lake (29)

This fishery lies adjacent to the Drumlish–Arvagh road. Annagh is quite a big lake that holds stocks of pike, perch, bream, roach, rudd and hybrids. Although I have never caught one myself, I was informed by a local farmer, that there are some big tench in the lake. Annagh is mainly weed-free around its very rocky shoreline.

Verdict

Well worth a visit, Annagh offers up plenty of easy shorefishing as well as a boat launching area. I have had pike of over 15lb from this fishery and I know anglers who have had some good pike sessions. Having said this, at times I have found the lake to be very moody with fruitless hours of fishing in pursuit of its pike. The bream fishing can also be slow, especially if you have not pre ground baited your swim, the bream grow large in Annagh and are hard fighters. This lake still offers up some good rudd fishing.

How to get there

We now have slightly different directions. This time approaching the Drumlish crossroads from the Longford road you travel straight on and out the Arvagh road for 5.9 miles where you meet the gate into the lake on your left at the small swimming pool complex. Go down behind this complex and keep right for plenty of shore fishing. Along this stretch you will be fishing into about eight to ten feet of water. If you keep up to the right you will come upon a bend on the shore line.

Out from this point I have had some good sessions of mainly bream rudd roach hybrids and perch. Sallagh averages 17 feet at its deepest point, which is in the

Annagh Lake, as seen from the road next to the amenity area. The North Longford Anglers' Club released 300 small pike into Annagh during July 2004.

middle of the lake. For boat launching area and more shorefishing go on for another 0.15 of a mile until you meet a narrow road into your left. Go down this road for 0.1 of a mile and you will see the boat launch on your left.

There is another place where you might get some excellent fishing. It's further up this narrow road, and directly out from the second row of conifer trees opposite the house. My fish finder showed up plenty of fish in this stretch of water, which averages ten to twelve feet. The fish finder also showed up a lot of fish near the bottom in the deepest part of the lake – this was during early August 2003. Photo of Lough Annagh on previous page.

NOTE:
> During July of 2004, the North Longford Anglers released 300 small pike into Lough Annagh. Over the past few years pike fishing on this lake has been very slow, so lets hope this stocking will bring Annagh back to its former glory.

Black Lake (30)

My advice on Black Lake is to stay away from it. No matter how much of an exploring angler you are. When I visited for the purposes of this book in August 2002, the lake was completely overgrown with weeds.

Verdict
The lane leading into the lake gets very steep and rough near the end, when I did reach the end there was nowhere to turn, so I had to reverse back up the hill. I can tell you it wasn't a pleasant experience, however if you want to fish a lake where probably no angler has ever fished before you could pay Black Lake a visit in early spring when the weed growth has yet to start.

How to get there
Approaching the Drumlish crossroads from the Longford road you go straight on out the Arvagh road for 9.1 miles until you meet the Moyne crossroads. Turn left here, go along for 0.6 of a mile and keep left at the Y-junction. Go up this road for 0.35 of a mile and take a right turn here. Go up the narrow lane for 0.4 of a mile to where you can park at the entrance to a blue roofed house. Do not attempt to drive down the steep hill. Walk down to the end of this lane, and continue into the fields and keep right to the rear of the wood where you will find the lake. If you make the journey, the best of luck!

Gulladoo Lough – Upp and Lower (31)
— The 10th Stepping Stone —

Next, we come to an excellent coarse fishery that is divided in the middle by a short stretch of river. I have had some nice sessions on this lake with bream, rudd, roach and hybrids. The pike fishing can also be first class. Gulladoo is well worth a visit with easy shore fishing and a boat launching area.

Verdict
Put Gulladoo on your short list and you will not be disappointed. I have found the upper lake the best, with plenty of double figure pike from this stretch as well as some nice bream, roach and hybrid sessions. Gulladoo can also offer up good tench fishing as well as the occasional big wild brown trout. There is a little folk village on the edge of the lake, this area is private property.

How to get there
Approaching the cross roads in Drumlish from the Longford road, go straight on through the village heading out the Arvagh road for 9.95 miles and turn left. Head up this road for 1.7 miles and turn left into area where the folk village is. On your way you will pass over the short stretch of river that divides the lake. Keep up to your left in this the lower part of Gulladoo where you will find plenty of easy shore fishing.

For shore fishing on the upper lake, instead of taking the left turn into the folk village, you keep straight on for 0.3 of a mile where you will find a way into the lake. At this point there is easy shore fishing. If you travel on from here for another 0.3 of a mile, you will find another gap on your left into the lake. Finally for a boat launching area and shore fishing off a wooden stand, just go on for 0.2 of a mile where you will see a parking area on your left into the lake. Best of luck.

This woman with her grandson are pictured enjoying a days fishing on Upper Gulladoo.

NOTE:

During August 2004, while on a visit to Upper Gulladoo, I met up with a British angler who was having a great bream and hybrid session on the lake. Luckily I had my video camera to record the occasion.

Mullandaragh Lough (32)

Another delightful little lake, which is surrounded by alder trees, I first visited Lough Mullandaragh in July 2001. It's with great joy that I can report seeing an otter swimming in the lake. It was nearly four years since I last saw an otter. I was beginning to wonder if there were any left in the wild. Let's hope this beautiful creature is left in peace to find a mate and increase the otter population.

Verdict

I am sorry to report Lough Mullandaragh has only a small area for shore fishing. The rest of the lake is surrounded by alder trees and high reeds with a very soft bank. A rubber dinghy would be the ideal way to fish this lake. There are local reports of good pike and bream fishing.

How to get there

Approaching the crossroads in Drumlish from the Longford road, you head straight out the Arvagh road for 9.1 miles, where you meet the Moyne crossroads. Turn left here and keep going for 0.5 of a mile where you meet a Y-junction. Keep right here. Go along this road for 2.45 miles, where you will meet a crossroads. Go straight on here until you meet a T-junction. You will now see the lake through

a gate down one field straight in front of you. Best of luck and keep an eye out for that otter.

Surrounded by alder trees, this fishery offers up only a small amount of difficult shore fishing. A rubber dinghy would be the best way to uncover the mysteries of Mullandaragh.

SAVE THE OTTER

Here in the Irish Midlands the otter has become very scarce. The last otter I witnessed was back in 2001 on Lough Mullandaragh, No. 32 in the Ten Stepping Stones. I realise this charming animal leads a secretive lifestyle, however for one who pays regular visits to local lakes and rivers, I would have expected to have encountered more otters on my travels.

I am delighted to say I have adopted an otter with the International Otter Survival Fund. The otter's name is SNOOPY and by all accounts is getting on very well. In the future, as more money becomes available from the sales of the books, I hope to be able to do more to help protect and care for this lovely playful animal of our wild countryside.

NOTE:
If any of the readers happen to see an otter here in the Irish Midlands, I would be delighted to hear about it. — Bernie

Snoopy

YOU CAN HELP US TO PRESERVE OTTERS

INTERNATIONAL OTTER SURVIVAL FUND

Broadford, Isle of Skye IV49 9AQ, Scotland
Tel/Fax: ++1471 822 487

Email: iosf@otter.org   Web page: www.otter.org   Charity No. SC003875

Town or Carrigallen Lough (33)

We are now coming to a fishery that caters well for the visiting angler. Carrigallen, or as it is sometimes called "The Town Lough", has a total of eight wooden stands. It is ideal for an easy day's fishing and because of this it is regularly fished. The lake is noted for its fabulous tench fishing, which grow extra large in this rather deep lake. The rudd, roach, perch and hybrids can be on the small size. There are also bream and pike present.

Verdict

What can I say, if you are in the area and looking for a comfortable day's fishing then the Town Lough is ideal. I've heard reports of some monster tench present in this delightful fishery. I have never been lucky enough to capture one – my heaviest weighed in at only 4lbs. When you arrive at the lake keep left for the wooden stands. You can also cross the stile on your right and this will lead you to some excellent shore fishing. Photos below, also pages 74 and 76.

How to get there

Approaching from the Longford road you head straight on at the crossroads in Drumlish and on out the Arvagh road for 9.1 miles until you meet the Moyne crossroads. Turn left here and go along for 0.5 of a mile until you get to the Y-junction. Turn right here and go along for 2.45 miles until you meet a crossroads where you turn right for Carrigallen. Keep on this road for 0.8 of a mile until you meet another Y crossing. Keep left here and travel 1.0 of a mile to the crossroads in Carrigallen town. Go left here for 0.15 of a mile and you will see a lane on your right with a "Town Lake" sign. Go down this narrow lane and there is plenty of car parking at the lake shore. For more shore fishing, instead of taking the left turn in Carrigallen town, you drive straight on for around 400

metres, where you will see a pass down to the lake. You can park over on your right. Tight Lines.

A really lovely scenic fishery. The Town Lough is noted for its large tench.

Gangin and Mosy's Loughs (34-35)

We now come to two delightful little fisheries. Gangin and Mosy's are close together and I presume offer up much the same sport for the angler. I have yet to fish these two lakes. On a visit for the purposes of this book. I found Gangin to be a dark muddy lake. I have no information on what coarse fish are present, however I would guess that Gangin holds both tench and bream.

Verdict

If you are in these parts do give Gangin a try. There are six wooden platforms and you can drive down through the fields to the lake shore where there is parking space. Remember to **close all the gates** after you enter. Go across the stile and keep left over two tree trunks. All the stands are on this side, on the opposite side of the lake there is a large rocky area, which offers up some good shore fishing. Mosy's Lough is over to the left behind Gangin. This fishery is heavily fringed with lily pads, which go out quite a distance into the lake. This can make fishing very difficult even from the wooden stands. Like Gangin, I would say Mosy's could also offer up some good bream and tench fishing.

How to get there

Gangin

Approaching from the Longford road you head straight on at the crossroads in Drumlish and out the Arvagh road for 9.1 miles until you meet the Moyne crossroads. Turn left here and go along for 0.5 of a mile until you get to the Y-junction. Turn right here and go along for 2.45 miles until you meet a cross-roads where you turn right for Carrig-allen. You will meet another Y-junction

Two delightful little lakes that lie close to Carrigallen. The lake in the foreground is Mosy's, while Gangin can be seen in the background.

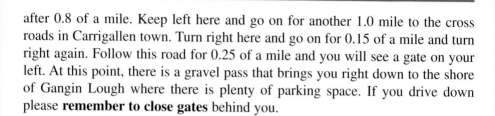

after 0.8 of a mile. Keep left here and go on for another 1.0 mile to the cross roads in Carrigallen town. Turn right here and go on for 0.15 of a mile and turn right again. Follow this road for 0.25 of a mile and you will see a gate on your left. At this point, there is a gravel pass that brings you right down to the shore of Gangin Lough where there is plenty of parking space. If you drive down please **remember to close gates** behind you.

Mosy's Lough

The directions to Mosy's are slightly different. When you arrive at the crossroads in Carrigallen town you turn right and go on for 0.45 of a mile where you take the right turn out the Arvagh road for 0.2 of a mile. At this point you will see a gap on your right into a field between some trees. Park here. To get to the lake, go through this gap and walk to your right along the hedge at the roadside, until you meet the next field. Go down this field and go through the gap, you will now see the lake. Keep over to your right and at end of the hedge you will find a wooden stile, cross over into next field where wooden stands are along lakeshore. Best of luck.

Lower Lough – or Hollybank (36)

Our final lake to visit in Area 3 is a splendid coarse fishery. Lower Lough or as it is called locally, Hollybank, offers up plenty of easy shore fishing. This lake is a must for the visiting angler. I have had some good fishing sessions on Hollybank, with bream, roach, rudd and hybrids as well as large perch and pike to the fore. The pike are excellent fighters, my biggest was taken on my first visit

back in the early 1970s. It weighed in at just under 20lbs and was taken on a small dead perch. Paddy highly recommends Hollybank for a visit.

A view down to Hollybank at the roadside sign for Arvagh. Note this is where Leinster, Ulster and Connaught meet.

Verdict

A must for the short list, with loads of comfortable shore fishing and plenty of fish, Lower Lough is a first class coarse fishery. There is parking place at the lakeshore. You just have to cross the wooden stile and walk up one field, then turn into your left where you will find all that easy shore fishing. There are no weeds growing along the edge of the lake, which also makes for easy fishing.

How to get there

Once again its back to the crossroads in Drumlish. Approaching from the Longford road, you head straight out the Arvagh road for 10.9 miles, at this point you can pull in at the gateway on your left. There is shore fishing at the end of this field. For more shore fishing, you must drive straight on for 0.4 of a mile into the town of Arvagh, this will bring you to the T-junction with Foster's Chemist shop straight in front. Turn left here and go up through the town passing the Breffni Arms Hotel on your left after 0.45 of a mile. You take the left turn here, which brings you down to the parking place. For the best shore fishing cross the wooden stile on your right and head up the field. Near the end of this field you turn left in to the lake where you will find all that comfortable shore fishing. I have found the shore up past the wooden stile at the edge of the lake to be the most productive. Hopefully, you will have a good day fishing. Best of luck.

NOTE:

During late July 2004, I paid a visit to Hollybank to get a photo of the lakeshore. When I arrived, to my surprise I found Longford angler Pat Mulryan along with his son and two British anglers fishing on the lake. They were having a great day fishing to mainly bream. Photo on page 77. The day prior to that, the two British anglers, Sean Ditchford and his son Robert had a great bream session on the lake with over 100lb of fish. On both days, the successful bait was maggot, ledgered about thirty to forty yards out. I noticed the green algae was prominent along the shore, however I was delighted it had no effect on the fish or fishing. In fact the discoloration of the water could have fooled the bream shoals into feeding during the daytime.

The Lock House

Recently refurbished and extended, this original Lock-keepers cottage is set in idyllic surroundings at the 41st Lock on the Royal Canal. It is close to Longford, Lanesboro, Athlone and Mullingar.

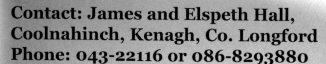

- Sleeps 4/5 persons.
- Fully equipped kitchen and laundry.
- All bedrooms ensuite.
- All bed linen and towels supplied.
- Special weekend rate available.
- Oil fired central heating.
- Turf fires available.
- A walker's paradise.
- Close to Corlea Heritage Centre and Mosstown stables.
- Top class coarse fishing on the Royal Canal.

**Contact: James and Elspeth Hall,
Coolnahinch, Kenagh, Co. Longford
Phone: 043-22116 or 086-8293880**
**Phone from outside Ireland
00-353-43-22116 or 00-353-86-8293880
E-mail: elspeth@iol.ie**

This photo shows the approach you will meet at the bridge in Roosky. This will be the starting-off point to the first seventeen lakes in the Ten Stepping Stones. Remember you will be approaching from the Longford road.

The second starting-off point is the crossroads in Drumlish. This photo shows what you will see, approaching from the Longford road. This starting-off point brings you to the last nineteen lakes in the Ten Stepping Stones.

This photo shows Foster's Pharmacy – the starting-off point to all sixteen lakes in the Breffni Quarter. You will be approaching from the Longford road.

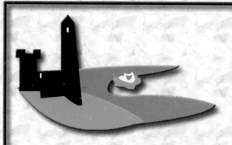

The Royal Canal

The three photos on this page show the quality of the tench in the Royal Canal. These fish were all caught by David O'Malley on sweetcorn during 2002.

The lower of the two tench on the bottom left was David's record fish at 9lb 3oz.

Paul Russell from Bristol in England with some lovely deep bodied wild Irish bream. These fish were taken during the summer of 2002 from Lough Cloonfinnan.

Me again with this close on 20lb pike taken during early spring 2003 on the Royal Canal where it meets the Shannon below Tarmonbarry.

Over 200lb of bream for Tony Egan and Tony Herbert. This catch was taken on Lough Sallagh, No. 20 in the Ten Stepping Stones, during the summer of 1997.

A tip from the master – Matt Hayes and I during the 2003 Angling Show in Birmingham. Despite his heavy work commitments during the show, Matt still found time to launch my first book. Matt is one nice guy.

Former Irish International pike angler, Joe McDermott, with two 20lb plus pike, taken from Lough Ree on a trolled dead roach. Joe's day fishing trip, during September 2003, produced a huge haul of six pike weighing in at an incredible 103lb.

RIGHT — British angler, Ian Young, with six nice tench taken on Creenagh Lake, No. 14 in the Ten Stepping Stones. Creenagh can be a difficult lake to have success on. Ian's catch was taken during the middle of April 2004.

BOTTOM LEFT — Max – my new German friend – doing a spot of pike fishing on Rinn Lough, No. 13 in the Ten Stepping Stones. Notice the walled gardens, part of Lough Rinn House estate in the background.

BOTTOM RIGHT — This is Tony (Scouser) Jones from Yorkshire in England with a decent Lough Gowna bream taken in September 2002. Lough Gowna is one of the best coarse fisheries in the Irish Midlands. I will be writing about this lake in Book 3.

That's me helping out with the release of 200 tench into Lough Sallagh, No. 20 in the Ten Stepping Stones. The Shannon Fishery Board were kind enough to transport the fish to the lake. This was during the summer of 2004. As far as I know these are the first tench to find their way into this fishery.

ABOVE — This visiting British angler ready to strike, on the shore of Lough McHugh. He gave me his name but I am sorry to say I mislaid it.

LEFT — Brian Bohan, sorting out his fabulous catch of twenty-eight tench from Lough Cloonfinnan, No. 6 in the Ten Stepping Stones. Note the one big bream on the right.

This view of the well-built wooden stands on this shore of the Town Lough in Carrigallen.

Lough Dernaweel – a mysterious fishery which is rarely if ever fished. Paddy and I are hoping to visit this lake to try and uncover its mysteries. Dernaweel is No. 5 in the Breffni Quarter.

Lough Rockfield, No. 6 in the Breffni Quarter. On the left you can see the lane that brings you into the alder avenue.

David Allison, with two nice bream from Lough Doogary, No. 24 in the Ten Stepping Stones. Note the lovely golden colours.

This visiting British angler with a nice roach from Gortinty Lake, No. 1 in the Ten Stepping Stones. Note all the easy shore fishing.

Another visiting British angler, this time on the shore of the Town Lough in Carrigallen, No. 33 in the Ten Stepping Stones. This decent tench was taken on a ledgered maggot and sweetcorn combination.

LEFT — Brian Bohan with a nice net full of golden rudd and two plump wild Irish tench. Taken from Drumbad Lake, No. 17 in the Ten Stepping Stones.

BELOW — Niall Mulryan with this bream taken on Hollybank Lough, No. 36 in the Ten Stepping Stones. On this particular day the bream were in a feeding frenzy. The successful bait was maggot, ledgered about thirty to forty metres out. Note all the easy shore fishing on this prime coarse fishery.

LEFT — This visiting Dublin angler, with what looks like a hybrid from Lough Aduff in Co. Leitrim, No. 2 in the Ten Stepping Stones. Note all the well-built wooden stands.

Breffni Arms Hotel
AND LEISURE CENTRE

In the heart of Ireland's Lakelands

THE BREFFNI ARMS HOTEL

Eamonn & Philomena Gray

Arvagh
Co Cavan
Eire
Tel: 049-4335127
Fax: 049-4335799
www.breffniarms.com
email: breffniarms@hotmail.com

Licensed Restaurant

Residential Bar

Function/Dance Hall

Indoor Swimming Pool

Sauna

Steam Room

Jacuzzi

Fitness Centre

The Breffni Arms is a newly refurbished family-run hotel and leisure centre. The hotel has twelve spacious bedrooms all with en-suite facilities including TV, phone, computer point, hair dryer and tea-making facilities. It nestles in an area famous for its golf courses, fishing lakes, horse riding and leisure walks. Also available locally: children's playground, tennis courts, pitch & putt and snooker.

RESTAURANT – Experience superb cuisine in the newly-decorated restaurant, or relax in the comfort of the hotel's main bar, where a wide choice of meals and drinks are available throughout the day.

ENTERTAINMENT – The large air-conditioned function / dance hall and bar offers an impressive setting and is perfect for weddings, banquets and other large events. There is live music on Fridays and Saturdays, and dancing to live bands on Sundays.

LEISURE CENTRE – The newly-appointed leisure centre has a fifteen metre indoor swimming pool, sauna, steam room, jacuzzi and a fully equipped fitness gymnasium, to make your stay even more memorable.

78

Cavan
One weekend
and you're hooked.

THE JOLLY BARMAN

THE GOURMET CHEF

THE UILEANN PIPER

Think of Cavan and you'll probably think
of lakes, rivers and fishing. And you'd be right
–with some of Ireland's finest inland waterways,
it offers the best of fishing all year round.

But, what else can you do?
Choose horse-trekking in Killykeen Forest Park
or hill-walking in the Cuilcagh Mountains.
Cruise the Shannon-Erne Waterway
and enjoy Cavan's riverside pubs and restaurants.

Come for a week or short break and
stay in a cottage, a castle, a farmhouse or log cabin.

And best of all, it's just a couple of hours away!

For more information call
North West Tourism
071 9161201
Cavan Tourism
049 4377200

NORTH WEST TOURISM

CAVAN
THE LAKE COUNTRY

79

Peter Newton from Yorkshire in England with a nice net full of mainly roach and hybrids, taken from Lough Gowna along Church shore. Many thanks Peter for all the kind help.

Brian Bohan with five nice plump wild Irish tench from Lough Errill, No. 5 in the Ten Stepping Stones. This can be a hard fishery to have success on, however, the rewards can be some unforgettable tench fishing.

A nice common carp for this visiting angler to Lakeland Fisheries.

A fabulous catch of well over 100lb of mainly bream from the mysterious Lough Clooncose in the North Longford border. These two visiting British anglers will remember this fishing trip.

Des McPartland, second from right, the owner of McPartland's Pub and Guesthouse in Clondra, Co. Longford, enjoying the company of these three visiting British anglers. "Paddy – the porter looks good"!

This photo taken during December 2003 shows John Ryan of the Shannon Fishery Board on left with resident English angler Brian Tabbiner. At the time, John was giving me a guided tour of the Suck River and its adjoining lakes. During this tour we met up with Brian at this stretch called Donamon. As a result of this visit I have decided to include this delightful fishery in Book 5. Hopefully I will be able to meet up with John and draw on his deep knowledge of this waterway.

Max – my new German friend

IT WAS back in the summer of 2002, just a few weeks after the publication of my first book, when I received a letter from a German angler by the name of Max. He wanted to purchase Book 1, which he saw advertised in the *Angling Ireland* magazine. Max is a keen pike angler and has been visiting the Strokestown area for over thirty years.

He first started to visit Ireland with his father. However, in recent years due to old age, Max's father has been unable to make the journey. Max and his family have a real love affair with the Irish Midlands.

When it comes to pike fishing, Max has a strict catch and release policy. In fact, I have seen few anglers who care more about the pike. He is most careful when unhooking a fish and is one of the best anglers I have witnessed performing this delicate operation.

After receiving my book, Max emailed me to find out if on his next visit I would be interested in going for a day's pike fishing. I emailed back and told Max to give me a ring when he was over here in Ireland, so we could arrange a day on one of the lakes.

Our first day's fishing together was on Lough Cloonfinnan. On the day we could only manage one pike of around 6lb, which Max took on a spoon bait. After the trip, Max asked me if I would be interested in going for another day's piking before he headed back to Germany. I told Max I would bring him up to Fin Lough, which is situated just outside Strokestown. Fin Lough is a noted tench fishery and has always thrown up some nice pike whenever I paid it a visit.

I met up with Max on Saturday at around 1.00pm. I remember the day well – the sky was clear with a very hot sun. We made our way over to Fin Lough, where we unloaded my boat *Adventurer*. The plan was to row around the lake trolling small dead perch and roach, and also using some artificial baits. At the time I had not purchased my electric engine. As I was the host, a little bit of pride was at stake, and I was hopeful that Max might have a good day's fishing with some double figure pike to the fore.

We must have fished for around four hours without as much as a bite. I rowed and rowed up and down the lake, pulling in along various weed beds where we ledgered dead bait on the bottom. We also float fished dead bait – all to no avail. The resident pike population were not interested in any of our offerings and the strong sunlight did not help.

Despite my best efforts and all my rowing for the best part of four hours, we were still fishless. I told Max it was time to call it a day, as I was rowing back towards the shore in a lather of sweat and a beaming hot sun baking down on me, Max in his broken English said "Bernie, me thought when me go fishing with you that me would catch plenty of big pike". I looked up at Max and broke out into a state of laughter. I just couldn't stop laughing.

Thankfully, since that day back in 2002, myself and Max have had some splendid days pike fishing here in his beloved Irish Midlands.

NOTE:
Here's a little tip that Max asked me to pass on. When he first started to visit Ireland, Max's father encouraged him to keep a diary of his day's pike fishing.

Max kept his main diary at home in Germany, when he went for a day's fishing he would write into a note book the amount of pike caught, their length and weight, the successful baits and methods used, the lake where they were caught, the time of day and year, prevailing weather conditions, and any other information that might be of interest.

When he returned to Germany, Max would carefully transfer all the details into his main diary. He told me that during the long winter nights he often takes out his diary, relaxes by the fire and lets all the fond memories of his Irish fishing trips to flow back. A nice way to spend a winter's night. Cheers Max.

Max with this small pike on Lough Cloonfinnan. This pike was taken on our first fishing trip together in 2002.

Paddy's Return to Nature

It was near the end of June1979, I was four years married at the time and had just moved a few miles from Longford town to my present home in Curry. On top of that, our first child was only 15 months old, so this was a very busy time in our family life.

I hadn't much contact with Paddy over the previous few months, so I decided to call to his house for a wee chat. When I arrived as usual the front door was wide open, in those days this was a common sight in the neighbourhood. I knocked at the door. There was a reply from Paddy's father who invited me in. I told him I was hoping to have a chat with Paddy, however he told me Paddy had gone off in his car a couple of days ago and he had not heard from him since. I asked Paddy's father if he had any idea where Paddy might be. "I'm not sure. The only clue I can give you is that he brought his dog and some of his camping gear with him," was Paddy's father's reply.

Over the years, myself and Paddy along with other friends in the neighbourhood went on regular camping trips to the local quarry, which was situated up a lane past the Bishop's house on the outskirts of Longford town. The quarry was an old derelict mining area that was used by the county council to extract stones for road making purposes. It was roughly the size of a football pitch and was about ten feet deep. The floor of the quarry was covered over with a fine layer of grass and was ideal for a campsite.

I decided that this area might be worth a try. On arrival I saw Paddy's car parked beside the gate, I pulled in alongside and made the rest of the journey on foot. On my way I noticed smoke rising from the quarry. As I got closer I could hear music playing. It was Paddy's favourite singer Jim Reeves whose voice was rising from Paddy's campsite. I gave a call "Is that you Paddy?" "Ah, Bernie you have found me, come on down and join me at the fire," was Paddy's reply.

There was a lovely little fire going. Over the fire on a spit Paddy was roasting a plump rabbit. "That's a fine rabbit," was my opening remark. "Captain caught him this morning in those whins at the edge of the quarry," said Paddy. Captain was Paddy's hunting dog and loyal companion. He was a great dog at finding rabbits. Paddy told me Captain was bred from a fox terrier bitch and his father was an Irish terrier.

I knew by Paddy there was something troubling him. "You don't seem yourself?" I asked. "Ah, you noticed Bernie," said Paddy. "I had better tell you what's on my mind or you will give me no peace. Do you remember that job I took in the local factory?" The previous autumn a new factory opened up in Longford town and was advertising for shift workers. At the time Paddy had never held down a full time job, he was of modest means and used to supplement his social welfare with the odd job working mainly for local farmers. There was a three shift system in the factory. Paddy saw this as an opportunity to purchase his first car and with the shift work he could get in plenty of fishing.

"For the first few months things went according to plan, I approached the bank manager and got a loan to purchase my first car a Volkswagen Beetle. The freedom this brought me was great at the time. I got in plenty of fishing and with you being so busy with family matters, it meant I could get to lakes that were too far to cycle to. However, Bernie, in recent times I am finding myself trapped in a way of life that seems to be getting more hectic as the weeks go by. As you know, before this I had no involvement with banks. My bicycle was my own, as well as any other bits and pieces that I possessed. I owed no money to any one and this gave me the freedom to live the way I wanted to. However, I am now finding there is pressure on me to work overtime to earn extra money to maintain the car and save for when I need to change it. This is causing me a lot of stress, as I am finding it harder and harder to get back to the simple things I enjoy like, fishing, gardening, hunting with Captain and generally being involved with nature.

Bernie, over the years you have always said a person's health is their wealth and peace of mind is their happiness. Right now, I am struggling with my peace of mind, so I have decided to take a break for a few days to clear my mind and give me the opportunity to think out what direction I want my life to move in. So, I decided to retreat to this quarry where I have always found great peace and happiness in the past". I appreciated Paddy's honesty and his predicament. The only words of comfort I could offer was to wish him well in whatever decision he came to. Paddy and I chatted on for a while. The pull of nature was beginning to get to me. How I would love to have stayed on with Paddy, chatting around that lovely cosy fire. I heard the sound of mallard ducks quacking overhead. Paddy told me they were regular visitors to the pond in the corner of the quarry. "The ducks are sharing the pond with two waterhens," said Paddy.

I had to go. My wife would be wondering where I got to and there was that never-ending lawn to cut. I bade farewell to Paddy, before heading back up the bank of the quarry and across the fields. As I took time to look back towards the campsite, I must say I was filled with a sense of joy at seeing Paddy sitting with Captain at his side and turning the rabbit on the spit. It was an unforgettable scene. I wondered to myself, what decision Paddy would come to. As I headed towards the car Paddy upped the volume of his tape recorder, filling the evening air with the sound of one of my favourite songs *Anna Marie*.

When I arrived home the chat with Paddy was bearing heavily on my mind. I started to think about my own life and the way it had become so hectic. I told my wife about my meeting with Paddy. We started to talk things over. I was considering working Saturdays to raise money to finance a new car and maybe have a foreign holiday. What happened that night was a change for the better in our family life. We decided to keep our weekends free, that new car could be done without and that holiday would have to fit in with our present means. My wife encouraged me to assure Paddy that I would be freer in the future, and we would be able to get in plenty of fishing trips together.

Paddy's Big Decision

It was a few days before I decided to visit Paddy. When I arrived at his house the door was closed and there was no sign of the car. I decided to head out as far as the quarry, on the way I had to pass alongside the Camlin River which is situated close to the road. As I was passing by, I spotted an angler on the bank of the river. I pulled in for a closer look. Sure enough, it was Paddy and sitting beside him was Captain. As I made my way towards them I noticed a plump brown trout of about 2lb and two nice sized eels lying beside Paddy on the riverbank. "You're having a nice day's fishing," I said to Paddy, "Oh hello Bernie, I captured them on the blackhead worm. That south wind is the fisherman's friend and with the cloudy sky it makes for ideal fishing conditions," said Paddy.

I was mad keen to find out what decision Paddy had come to. In fact I was so eager I failed to notice there was no sign of Paddy's car. After a few minutes, Paddy invited me to accompany him to where the old bridge use to cross the river. He had spotted a nice trout moving in this stretch of the Camlin earlier in the day, and now wanted to give it a try. On our way, Captain was busy showing

off his hunting skills – first bolting a rabbit out of a hedge. The rabbit won the day escaping to the safety of his burrow before Captain could close in. Further along the river Captain's hunting skills were again to the fore, flushing a water rat from the long grass at the edge of the river. With an almighty splash Captain jumped into the river in pursuit of the rat. Paddy started shouting: "Good boy Captain! You show him who is the boss!" However, the rat's ability to swim under water was too puzzling for Captain who wasn't long in giving up the chase.

As we approached the remains of the old bridge, Paddy ordered Captain to heel. It was now Paddy's time to do the hunting. He pointed out a deep hole that was just below the bridge on our side of the river. "Bernie, I bet that's where that trout is holding up. I will cast my worm just up stream of it and allow the worm to be washed nice and naturally into the hole," said Paddy.

Paddy cast the worm upstream with almost pin-point accuracy and allowed it to be washed back into the hole. With the worm now resting on the bed of the river, Paddy put his rod down and waited to see if the trout would be in a taking mood. "Well Bernie, I suppose you are wondering what decision I have come to?" asked Paddy. "To tell you the truth that is the main reason I came looking for you," I told Paddy. "After a lot of thinking on the matter I decided to quit the job, I sold the car and with the money I received I called to the bank manager and paid off the remainder of the loan. I am now back to where I was before taking the job. I have no loans and no financial worries, so I can now go fishing whenever I want. Maybe Bernie I am just a drop-out or too lazy to work, however I feel I have made the right decision," said Paddy.

"Well Paddy, I have done a lot of thinking myself. In future I'm making sure that I also have more free time to follow my favourite pastime." "Bernie does that mean we will be going on regular fishing trips together?" asked Paddy. "You can be sure of that," I said. With the knowledge and delight of knowing Paddy's decision, I bade farewell to Paddy and Captain and headed back to the car. On the way, I thought to myself – to live a simple life is a gift and to live a simple life with strength is a blessing. No Paddy – you are not a drop-out and you are not lazy – you have followed your heart – you are a true man of nature.

Map of Area 4

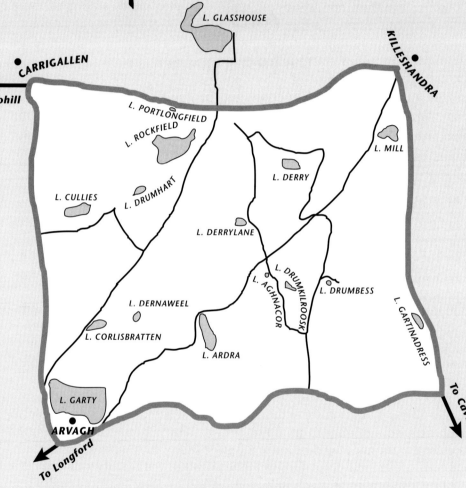

L. GLASSHOUSE

KILLESHANDRA

CARRIGALLEN

Mohill

L. PORTLONGFIELD

L. ROCKFIELD

L. MILL

L. DERRY

L. CULLIES

L. DRUMHART

L. DERRYLANE

L. DRUMKILROOSK

L. DRUMBESS

L. ACHNACOR

L. DERNAWEEL

L. GARTINADRESS

L. CORLISBRATTEN

L. ARDRA

To Cavan

L. GARTY

ARVAGH

To Longford

The Breffni Quarter

An Anglers Guide to Coarse Fisheries in the Irish Midlands

AREA 4

The Breffni Quarter

Welcome along to Area 4, I hope your journey through the Ten Stepping Stones was informative and enjoyable. I am calling Area 4 "The Breffni Quarter". With just sixteen lakes, it is the smallest area we will be visiting in the Irish Midlands. However despite its small size, The Breffni Quarter holds some first class coarse fisheries.

I bet you are wondering where I got the name – The Breffni Quarter – let me explain. In Arvagh town, (which will be the starting-off point for all sixteen fisheries) the local hotel has proved to be a really warm and welcoming alehouse for both myself and Paddy and other visiting anglers. We have enjoyed many the great nights' craic in its friendly bar. The name of this hotel is The Breffni Arms.

So there you have the first part of the name explained. As to the second part – well there are sixteen lakes in Area 4, if you divide 16 by 4 you get 4 – which is a quarter, this area is also called Area 4, and finally if you look at the map of Area 4 you will see it in the shape of a square with 4 corners. There you have it – my reason for calling Area 4 The Breffni Quarter.

After all that let's get down to the real business at hand – exploring all those 16 fisheries, we start off with the Town Lough – Garty. I feel this lake has great potential to become a top class coarse and game fishery. Next we have Corlisbratten, another one of those delightful small fisheries where you can enjoy an easy day's fishing to mainly, perch, roach, rudd and hybrids. Then there's Cullies Lough where Paddy discovered its nice bream and tench fishing over a game of 25 in the Breffni Arms Hotel. Dernaweel is a lovely wild and scenic fishery that is definitely for the exploring angler. When I first discovered Dernaweel I was enchanted by its natural wild location. Since then this picturesque lake has been constantly on my mind. I have a feeling Dernaweel could be a first class coarse fishery.

Drumkilroosk is another lake for the exploring angler. A wild fishery that offers up plenty of shore fishing. My fisherman's instinct tells me that this could be a fabulous bream and tench lake. Lough Gartinardress, with its fishing stands tucked away at the edge of a wooded shoreline, looks like another top class coarse fishery. Glasshouse Lake, going by reports from visiting British anglers could be a gem of a coarse fishery, and then there is Mill Lough, a noted pike fishery that is set in lovely scenic surroundings.

These are just some of the fisheries for us to visit in the Breffni Quarter, there are sixteen in all, here is the order in which we will be visiting them:

1. Lough Garty
2. Lough Cullies
3. Lough Drumhart
4. Lough Corlisbratten
5. Lough Dernaweel
6. Lough Rockfield
7. Lough Portlongfield
8. Lough Glasshouse
9. Lough Ardra
10. Lough Derrylane
11. Lough Derrylough or Creenagh
12. Lough Aghnacor
13. Lough Drumkilroosk
14. Lough Drumbess
15. Lough Mill or Portaliffe
16. Lough Gartinardress

How to get there
For directions to all sixteen fisheries in The Breffni Quarter we will be using the T-junction in Arvagh town with Foster's chemist shop straight in front (as can be seen in photo on page 67) as the starting off point, remembering that we will be approaching from the Longford road. When you meet Arvagh town keep left, this will bring you up to Foster's chemist shop.

Lough Garty (1)

As we start out on our journey through the Breffni Quarter, the first fishery we encounter is Garty Lough, often known as the Town Lough. This fishery lies alongside the town of Arvagh.

Garty offers up plenty of easy shore fishing as well as a boat launching area. The lake lies just fifty metres off the main road in the town of Arvagh and fishing is into fairly deep water. The water quality of Garty is very good as can be seen from the little stream that runs out of the lake and under the road in Arvagh town.

Verdict

I have a feeling Garty is just waiting to be developed into a top class coarse and game fishery. It has plenty of the right ingredients – excellent water quality, good variation in its depths (going down to over forty feet at its deepest). A nice tributary river and situated in the heart of Arvagh town. With proper management, this fishery could become a big attraction for visiting coarse and game anglers, and give a much-needed boost to local tourism.

How to get there

Approaching Arvagh town from the Longford road, you drive straight up to T-junction with Foster's chemist shop in front. Take a left turn here. Proceed up through the town with the Breffni Arms Hotel on your left for just 0.1 of a mile until you see a right turn into the lake. For the best shore fishing keep right over the small river. You can travel along this shore for quite a journey. The fishing is into fifteen to twenty-five feet of water. Be careful along this shore when wading as the lake suddenly drops to eleven feet. At its deepest Garty goes down to forty-two feet which is in the middle of the lake. There is an easy boat launching area at the shore of the lake.

Cullies Lough (2)

We now come to one of my favourite coarse fisheries in the Breffni Quarter. Cullies Lough is a real gem. It offers up bream, tench, rudd, roach, hybrids, perch, pike and eel fishing. I highly rec-ommend this lake for a visit. Cullie also offers up easy shore fishing into mainly weed-free water.

Yorkshire angler, Glyn Wydell, along the rocky shoreline of Cullies Lough. Story of Paddy and me on our first visit to this scenic fishery is on page 93.

Lake in the Valley

It was in the mid nineteen eighties when Paddy and myself first found out about this delightful fishery. After a day fishing on Corlisbratten we were heading home through Arvagh town when Paddy started to complain about the thirst – nothing would do him but a quick pint in the Breffni Arms Hotel. As usual, Paddy's powers of persuasion won the day. I pulled up outside the hotel telling him I could only entertain one pint. "No problem Bernie, we will soon be on our way" – Paddy's famous words over the years. The Breffni Arms holds fond memories for Paddy and I. The hotel has a nice relaxing bar where fishermen are always welcome. On this particular evening, we found the bar was empty on our arrival. Paddy ordered two pints and we settled into conversation about our day's fishing on Corlisbratten. After about half an hour we were nearing the end of our drinks. I asked Paddy to drink up so we could be on our way. Just then three anglers arrived. Paddy seized the opportunity. "Any luck today lads?" he inquired. "We had a good bream and tench session on Cullies Lough" was the reply. At that time we knew nothing about this lake. Paddy's curiosity was aroused "Great area around here for coarse fishing, we just had a nice roach, rudd and hybrid session ourselves on Corlisbratten" was Paddy's reply. One of the visiting anglers took the bait "is that far from here?" he asked. "No, just a couple of miles. There are plenty of wooden stands on the lake which is just one field off the road," said Paddy. "We're heading back home tomorrow. On our next visit we must try this fishery," said the visitor.

Paddy was quick to enquire further about Cullies. "You encountered some nice bream and tench. Is there much shore-fishing?" asked Paddy. "Plenty of easy shore-fishing up around the rocky shoreline," was the reply. This bit of willing information helped Paddy to relax. His next question was the obvious one. "How do you get to Cullies?" "It's not far. You head out the Carrigallen road for about two and a half miles, turn right there and keep on for around a half a mile where you will see a gate on your left. If you go in at this gate, you will see the **Lake in the Valley**, at the bottom of the steep hill."

Paddy turned to me, "Now Bernie, we have a new fishery to try. These look like a nice bunch of lads – do you mind if I have one more pint with them?" asked Paddy. I looked around the table. All eyes were on me. Not wanting to appear like a spoilsport, I told Paddy he could have one more. This statement brought about a new atmosphere. There was the sense of a session in the air. As it was

their last night, I could see by the visiting anglers they were planning to have a good night in the bar.

I was in a bit of a dilemma, if I drank one more pint, myself and Paddy would have to order a taxi, as I never drive if I'm over the limit. Paddy sensed my dilemma. "Bernie, why don't you phone your wife and ask her could you stay overnight in the Breffni Arms, I'll pay the cost of the bed and breakfast, and we can head out early in the morning to this new fishery. You said your wife's sister is staying for the weekend, so this might be a good opportunity," said Paddy.

Late Session

Paddy is never slow when it comes to finding excuses for a session. I went out to the lounge to make the phone call, my fingers were crossed. "Hello Phil, I'm here in the Breffni Arms Hotel having a drink with Paddy and some visiting British anglers. They were telling us about an exciting new fishery called Cullies Lough. I was wondering would you mind if myself and Paddy stayed over for the night in the hotel, so we can head out first thing in the morning to fish the lake." "Now Bernie what about the painting and gardening jobs you promised to do this weekend," said Phil. I had to think fast, "Well Paddy has promised to help me, we'll be home early tomorrow morning, and myself and Paddy will start into those jobs straight away". There was total silence, I thought she was going to hang up, I jumped in with an offer. "Phil, I will also treat yourself and your sister to a meal and a night out." This offer did the trick. "OK Bernie, make sure you behave yourself and be home first thing tomorrow morning," said Phil.

I rushed back into the bar to tell Paddy the good news, when I arrived, I found Paddy and the other three anglers engrossed in a game of cards. "You were fairly sure of yourself," I quipped to Paddy. "Yes we can stay the night, however, I told Phil we would be back home early in the morning." "No problem," said Paddy. "Now take a seat and join us in this game of 25." We played cards and drank porter. The craic was mighty as both Paddy and one of the British anglers exchanged jokes over the game of cards. It was after midnight when I told Paddy I was retiring. At this stage, Paddy had won a few pounds and I knew by him that he was hoping to recoup the price of the bed and breakfast. As I was leaving Paddy said, "There's no need to worry about sleeping in. I'll give your door a knock when it's time to get up."

Our plan was to be at the lake about an hour and a half before daybreak. During the warm summer months, we have found the hour before dawn and one hour after, as well as the hour before nightfall, and the hour after are the best times to catch those wild Irish bream and tench. As the visiting anglers had heavily ground-baited the lake at the rocky shoreline for the previous few days, it was important that we fished it as soon as possible while the shoals of bream were heading over to this area in search of the easy offerings.

I was in a deep sleep when a knock at the door woke me. "Is that you Paddy?" I asked. "Yes Bernie, it's time to get up, we'll have to hurry if we are to make it to the lake on time," said Paddy. In fairness to the British anglers their guidance was spot on, we made our way down the steep hill to the lake where we found plenty of parking place. After unloading our gear, I used my torch to find our way through the wood and up to the rocky shoreline. It was still dark when we set up our tackle. I mentioned to Paddy that we would have to go easy on the maggots, as there weren't many left. "No need to worry Bernie, I got a full box from the British anglers," said Paddy. As it was still fairly dark we used the old reliable silver paper as our bite indicator. It was not long before Paddy had a run – a bream of about 4lbs for openers. He was quickly into action again, this time a hybrid near the 2lb mark. For the next hour, we were kept busy with fish coming to the net on a regular basis.

The dawn was now breaking. It's one of my most treasured moments in nature, relaxing by the side of a lake, observing the rays from the early morning sun as they slowly move across the landscape, and thanking God for the gift of another new day. As the mist lifted off the water, it revealed two swans with three cygnets observing us from the middle of the lake. Overhead a flock of mallards were heading home after their night's feeding. When they spotted Paddy and I they quickly veered off, circling the upper end of the lake before gliding into the reeds. Over at the edge of the lily pads two waterhens were making their presence felt as they noisily went about their early morning work. Nature was starting to wake up. As I sat back in the still morning air, I started to imagine what it must be like down there in that watery domain. If only for a short time I could change into a fish, and slide under the surface to join the other inhabitants. How I would love to observe in particular the feeding habits and movements of the resident bream and tench population. However, maybe it is for the best that these wild Irish fish are still able to keep some secrets from the visiting angler.

Otters — Water Snake

Fish were still coming to the net. We had a nice bag of mainly, bream, roach, rudd, hybrids and perch, with some nice tench for good measure. I called to Paddy, "With all these fodder fish about, I bet there is a big pike lurking out there." Paddy was thinking along the same lines, "Bernie I'll head up to the car to get my pike rod." As Paddy was heading back to the car, I noticed activity along the far shoreline. It looked like a pair of otters out hunting for an early morning breakfast. I rushed after Paddy to tell him to fetch my pair of binoculars from the back seat of the car.

When Paddy arrived back, there was no sign of the otters, I decided to give the fishing a break while I kept a close watch for one of my favourite animals. Paddy had set up his pike rod and was fishing a ledgered dead roach about forty yards out. After about ten minutes, I spotted a brown shape moving through the water. Sure enough, it was an otter. I kept a close watch through my binoculars, observing this graceful animal at work searching out his watery habitat for fish, crayfish, eels, and any other snack bits that might come his way.

Paddy broke the silence, "Bernie my silver paper is on the move, could be another bream," I said. "No Bernie, it's my pike rod". With that Paddy slowly lifted the rod before striking. "Are you in?" I shouted. "Yes Bernie, it's a good fish, he's holding tight to the bottom. I will have to exert a lot more pressure if I am to move him," said Paddy. With one almighty heave, Paddy managed to move the fish off the bottom. "I have him on the move, he's doing a lot of wobbling. Hey Bernie, I think it's a water snake," (Paddy's name for an eel). Sure enough, Paddy had caught a nice eel of just over 2lb. "This one is for the pan," said Paddy. Fried eel is a favourite with Paddy who is skilled in the art of skinning them. Paddy holds great faith in the healing power of an eels skin for sprains and other hurts to the joints and muscles.

Paddy's Surprise

We decided to call it a day, besides the eel our morning's work provided us with almost 70lb of bream, roach, rudd, hybrids, perch and tench. The sun was now shining bright. It was a beautiful morning. I thanked God for giving me the health and wisdom to enjoy these free gifts of nature. I also thought of those three British anglers who were so forthcoming in their information and advice about the, **'Lake in the Valley'**.

On our way home to Longford, we had to take a sharp right turn in Arvagh town, just pass the Breffni Arms Hotel. When we approached the turn Paddy asked me to pull in so we could have our breakfast. I told him I promised Phil I would be home early. On our way out of the town Paddy said, "Bernie, when we are approaching Longford, would you mind dropping me off out the Bishop's road near the old racecourse. This looks like a good morning for picking mushrooms. Fried eels and mushrooms will make a hearty breakfast." I pulled in at the side of the road, Paddy enquired if there was something wrong. "No Paddy I have changed my mind, that big Irish breakfast in the Breffni Arms will set us up nicely for the gardening and painting jobs that are facing us." Paddy was quick to reply, "Bernie, what do you mean by **US!**?"

How to get there
Approaching Arvagh town from the Longford road, you drive straight up to the T-junction with Foster's chemist shop straight in front. Take the left turn here and proceed up through the town with Breffni Arms on your left. Drive on for 2.5 miles where you will meet a right turn. Go up this road for 0.4 of a mile. At this point you will see a gate on your left. Go through this gateway to the next gate. You now have to drive down a steep hill to the parking area at the edge of the lake (**remember to close both gates after you enter**). Straight in front of the parking area, the lane leads you down to the edge of the lake where you can launch a boat. This part of the lake can be a hot spot for tench. On your right you will see a wood. When you enter this wood, you will find some nice shore fishing. If you head up to the end of the wood, you will see the rocky shoreline where Paddy and I had that delightful early morning's fishing on **the Lake in the Valley**. Photo of Cullies Lough on page 92.

"Hi Bernie."
"Yes Paddy."

"Do you want a tip on how to make your lawn easy to maintain?"
"Yes Paddy."

"During the month of February, get two pints of beer and mix it in with ten gallons of water. Pour the mixture into a watering can and sprinkle it over your lawn."
"Paddy how will this make a lawn easy to maintain?"

"Well Bernie when the grass starts to grow it will come up half cut."
"Good man Paddy."

Drumhart Lough (3)

Shore fishing is limited on this small fishery. I have yet to fish Drumhart and can only pass on information from two visits for the purposes of this book. On my first visit I made the journey down through the fields. At this time the part of the lake I came upon had a very soft shoreline which was overgrown with tall reeds. I was going to report the lake as one for the exploring angler who would need a rubbery dinghy. However, on my second visit via the small river which enters Lough Rockfield, I found some shore fishing on Drumhart near to where the river leaves the lake.

Verdict
Most definitely for the exploring angler, the lake lies about 600 metres down the fields. When I visited the lake in my boat *Adventurer* during late March 2004 the fish finder showed small concentrations of fish. On this occasion, most of the fish were shoaling near to where the river leaves the lake. It is along this area where shore fishing is possible. You will be fishing into five to eight feet of water. At its deepest Drumhart goes down to nine feet.

How to get there
Approaching Arvagh town from the Longford road, you drive straight up to the T-junction with Foster's chemist shop in front. Turn left here and drive on past the Breffni Arms Hotel which is on your left. Keep going for 2.5 miles until you meet a right turn. Go up this road for 1.55 miles, take the left turn here and go on for 0.2 miles where you keep right. Drive along this road for 0.8 of a mile until you see a right turn into a narrow road. Take this, go up it for 0.1 of mile where you keep right. Keep going for another 0.3 of a mile and then you can park near a gate on your right with a house on your left. Go through the gate and down some steep fields to where the lake lies approximately 600 metres away. For shore fishing, when you are heading down the field you will see two trees. Keep over to the left of these trees and head into the rushy field. You must go through this rushy field and into the next field where you will find shore fishing near to where the river leaves the lake. You could also make the short journey by boat from Rockfield. (**Please remember to ask permission at the house if you make the journey.**) Best of luck.

Corlisbratten Lough (4)

We are now visiting a delightful little coarse fishery with easy access. Corlisbratten is one of my favourite lakes in Area 4. I have had some enjoyable sessions, mainly to perch, rudd, roach and hybrids. There are three wooden stands on the lake, however, the middle one is in need of repair.

Verdict
Corlisbratten rests down in a valley and is a lovely scenic lake. Paddy and myself love paying it a visit, we always enjoy the occasion with a mixed catch mainly of roach, rudd, hybrids and perch. On a recent visit I noticed a young chestnut tree growing beside the wooden stand on the left. Keep an eye out for it. There is also some shore fishing on this delightful fishery.

How to get there
Approaching Arvagh town from the Longford road, you drive straight up to the T-junction with Foster's chemist shop in front. Take the left turn and proceed up through the town with the Breffni Arms Hotel on your left for 0.5 of a mile. Take the right turn here and keep going along this road for 1.4 miles where you will see a gate on your right into the lake. Tight Lines.

NOTE:

During March 2004, I went to visit Corlisbratten, to do some videoing. When I arrived, I found four newly built wooden stands at the lakeshore.

Access to these stands is one field down.

A view down to the new wooden stands on Corlisbratten. The older stands are up to the left.

Lough Dernaweel (5)

We now come to a truly mysterious lake that has rarely been fished. There is only one place where you can get some shore fishing on Lough Dernaweel. It is a small area where the local farmer has made a stony pass into the lakeshore to enable his live stock to get a drink. I have absolutely no information whatsoever about Dernaweel. The lake is set in lovely scenic surroundings and miles off the beaten track. If you want to go where very few angler's have fished before, then Dernaweel could be for you.

Verdict
When I visited Dernaweel in July of 2001, I had to walk nearly a mile along a rough laneway and then down three fields to get to the lake. I must say it was love at first sight. I just couldn't believe such a lovely scenic fishery was about to come into view. From the shore the lake immediately drops off into dark deep water. High reeds and lily pads surround Dernaweel. Once again it is my fisherman's instinct, but I think this is one fabulous fishery. From the way the surrounding landscape drops steeply towards the lake, I'd say Dernaweel is a very deep lake. Maybe some day, God willing, Paddy and myself might make our way to Dernaweel and uncover its mysteries in our rubber dinghy *Explorer*.

How to get there
Approaching Arvagh town from the Longford road, you drive straight up to T-junction with Foster's chemist shop in front. Take the left turn and keep going past the Breffni Arms Hotel (which is on your left) for 0.5 of a mile. At this point you take the right turn. Go along this road for 2.1 miles where you will see a lane in to your right. Go up this lane for 0.1 of a mile and park on the grassy bank on your right. You must walk along this rough laneway for nearly a mile where you will see the lake three fields down straight in front. If you're driving a 4-wheel drive then you might be able to drive down to this point. Next make your way down through the fields and look for the stony pass into the lakeshore. This is the only area for shore fishing. If you were brave enough to make the journey then the best of luck – you deserve it!

NOTE:
On a visit during 2003, when I was videoing Lough Dernaweel, the laneway down to the lake had been recently resurfaced for about three-quarters of the way.

Lough Rockfield (6)

We are now visiting a large lake that provides plenty of easy shore fishing, Lough Rockfield is definitely for the short list when you are visiting these parts. I have had some nice fishing both from my boat and off the shore. The bream are extra large, while there is also good roach, rudd, hybrid, perch and pike fishing. There are reports of big wild brown trout present in this delightful fishery. At the point where the road meets the lake, you will be fishing into seventeen to twenty feet of water. Along the Alder Avenue, the lake drops off suddenly, to a depth of between ten and seventeen feet. Up to the right of the roadway, Rockfield gets very shallow, in places only going to a depth of two to four feet. At its deepest, which is directly out from the roadway, the lake goes down to thirty-eight feet.

Verdict
Rockfield is well worth a visit. The Alder Avenue on your left when you meet the lake is often the most productive shoreline. My biggest pike from Rockfield weighed in at 18lbs 6ozs, and was taken off this shoreline using dead roach as bait. In the past this fishery has produced fabulous bream fishing, however as with a lot of the lakes in the Irish Midlands the bream shoals are now becoming harder to locate. On a visit during April of 2004, when I was doing a spot of pike fishing from my boat *Adventurer*, the fishfinder showed up a lot of fish out in the centre of the lake. These fish were mainly lying near the bottom in over thirty feet of water. I have discovered this trend on a lot of the lakes.

How to get there
Approaching Arvagh town from the Longford road, you drive straight up to the T-junction with Foster's chemist shop in front, turn left here and go up this road with Breffni Arms Hotel on your left for 0.5 of a mile and take the right turn. Go along this road for 3.5 miles where you will see a left turn with a sign for the lake on your left. Go down this very narrow road until you meet the lake. If you meet another car someone will have to reverse back. At the lake shore you will see Alder Avenue on your left (area through wood of alder trees). The shoreline along this part of the lake usually proves most productive. A boat can be launched from this area. Best of luck. (Photo of Rockfield on page 74)

NOTE:

During May of 2004, Chas Tarry visited Lough Rockfield and found that the steep hill on the way down to the lake had been recently covered over with stones. This made the approach almost impossible, and he was very lucky to be able to drive back up the hill. Hopefully the Council will have tarred over the stones by the time you read this.

Lough Portlongfield (7)

I have fished Portlongfield on a few occasions. It is one of those small fisheries where you are assured of a hectic day's fishing to mainly small roach, rudd and hybrids. Portlongfield is a lovely little lake that lies just off the main road.

Verdict

If you are fishing some of the larger lakes in this area and finding the fish hard to come by then nip over to Portlongfield. You can expect your confidence to be restored with all those lovely little roach and rudd mad eager to accept your offering and who knows if you ledger a lobworm what little delights are lurking on the bed of this pleasant little fishery?

How to get there

Approaching Arvagh town from the Longford road, you drive straight up to the T-junction with Foster's chemist shop in front. Take the left turn and proceed up through the town with the Breffni Arms Hotel on your left for 0.5 of a mile. Take the right turn here, keep going for 4.25 miles until you meet a crossroads and go left here. Continue along this road for another 0.6 of a mile where you can park at the lane on your right. The entrance to the lake is fifty metres up on your left side. Head straight down between the gap in the bushes for shore fishing. The lake is hidden behind high rushes. Tight Lines.

A small fishery for an easy day's fishing. Portlongfield holds plentiful stocks of small fish.

Glasshouse Lake (8)

Glasshouse Lough lies just on the edge of the Breffni Quarter. I have decided to include it mainly because of the praise that visiting anglers have bestowed on it. This fishery offers up loads of easy shore-fishing which is weed-free and situated close to the parking area. I have not fished Glasshouse, however I recommended it to British angler Chas Tarry as a good fishery for his friend Bill who is a disabled angler. On a visit in May 2004, they fished the lake for two consecutive days without as much as a bite. Why this should be so I honestly do not know. Maybe the coarse fish were off spawning in some other section of the lake or in some of the lakes close by which are easily negotiated via a small river.

Verdict
On what I thought was my first visit to Glasshouse. I in fact ended up on Lough Derreskit, a nearby lake. This was during the middle of the day in late July 2003. There were four British anglers on the shore of Derreskit. They had a good day's catch to mainly large roach, skimmers and hybrids. Photo on page 104.

I decided during early spring of 2004 to revisit Glasshouse with my boat *Adventurer* and explore the lake to find out its depths, shore fishing, and also to do some videoing. When I arrived at Derreskit which I thought was Glasshouse, I found the gate into the lake locked, so I turned around and started to head for home. On my travels I meet up with a local who told me that the lake I was visiting was not Glasshouse – and that this lake was further back up the road and down a lane to my right.

Plenty of easy shore fishing – ideal for the disabled angler, but I am wondering how good a coarse fishery Glasshouse Lough is.

So there you have it, I was lucky to have made the return visit. If I had not, I would now be guiding you to the wrong lake. If you would like to pay Derreskit a visit, instead of taking the final left turn into Glasshouse you drive straight on for another 0.6 of a mile. At this point you will see a gate on your left. When you drive in here, go down through the first field and then drive to the end of the second field, where you will find plenty of easy shore fishing. If the gate is locked, you can enquire locally for the owner who might unlock it for you.

How to get there
Approaching Arvagh town from the Longford road, you drive straight up to the T-junction with Foster's chemist shop in front. Turn left here and proceed up through the town with the Breffni Arms Hotel on your left for 0.5 of a mile, turn right here and go along this road for 4.25 miles. At this point, you will meet a crossroads. Remembering to give right of way, you go straight on for 0.6 of a mile, where you take the right turn. Head up this road for 0.2 of a mile, where you will see a lane on your left. Drive up this lane for 0.2 of a mile where you will meet a gate into the lake on your left. There is plenty of easy shore fishing on this side of the lake. For more shore fishing, instead of turning left into the lake, you drive further along the lane for 0.3 of a mile till you meet the end of a stony road, with a new two-storey house on your right. You can park in this area and the lake is on your left. If you walk straight on, you will find plenty of shore fishing between gaps in trees at the side of the lake. Glasshouse varies considerably in depth, at its deepest the lake goes down to over thirty feet. Along the shore you will be fishing into between eleven to fifteen feet of water. The lake has a mainly stony bottom which is weed-free. Tight Lines.

These British anglers enjoying their days fishing on Lough Derreskit. This is the lake I found by mistake while looking for Glasshouse Lough.

Lough Ardra (9)

We now come to a very interesting fishery. I have never fished Lough Ardra and have no information to pass on. From my own observations, I would say it could offer up good bream, rudd, roach and hybrid fishing. There is a small stream, which leaves Ardra and heads down to Lough Garty, in heavy floods fish could quite easily travel between both lakes.

Verdict
Lough Ardra lies close to the roadway and could be well worth a visit. It is a long narrow straggling fishery. There is a limited amount of shore fishing in two different parts of the lake. Despite being located so close to the road, I have a feeling Lough Ardra is rarely fished. A rubber dinghy would be ideal for finding out its mysteries.

How to get there
We are now following slightly different directions: Approaching Arvagh town from the Longford road, you still drive up to the T-junction with Foster's chemist shop straight in front. Now we must take a right turn and drive up through the town for 0.3 of a mile where we keep left. Go on for a further 0.3 of a mile where you should also take the left turn. After another 0.45 of a mile, you meet a junction. Turn left here and head out the Killeshandra road. Follow this road for 1.95 miles where you will see a pretty bungalow on your right. Park at the gate on the right just down the road from the house. Go down the fields towards the lake and turn right near the lake for shore fishing. If you drive on for 0.15 of a

mile, you will see a gate into your right. You can go down this field to the lake for more shore fishing. **Please remember to ask at the house for permission to go down through the fields.**

This is a view of Lough Ardra from the road – a mysterious fishery.

Lough Derrylane (10)

We are now visiting a very dark and murky lake. I have no reports about Derrylane and have yet to fish it. This small lake, which lies just 200 metres from the road, offers up plenty of easy shore fishing.

Verdict
Lough Derrylane could be anything. I honestly do not know what to make of it, if you are interested in paying it a visit then by all means give it a try and who knows what you might uncover.

How to get there
Approaching Arvagh town from the Longford road, you drive straight up as far as the T-junction with Foster's chemist shop in front. Turn right here and keep going for 0.3 of a mile where you keep left. Go on for a further 0.3 of a mile where you should also take the left turn. After another 0.45 of a mile, you meet a junction. Turn left here and head out the Killeshandra road. Keep going for 3.55 miles and then take the left turn at the crossroads. Drive on for 0.6 of a mile and park at the gate on your left. The lake is just down the field.

This small fishery is a total mystery to me. If you do fish Derrylane, please let me know how you got on.

Derrylough or Creenagh (11)

We now come to a nice scenic fishery, Derrylough or as it is often called locally, Creenagh, is well worth a visit. There is lots of shore fishing and a boat can be easily launched. I have fished this lake on only two occasions, both times I enjoyed my visit and had respectable catches of 50lb plus of bream, roach, rudd and hybrids. If my memory serves me right the heaviest bream weighed in at just under 5lbs.

Verdict
This could be an exciting bream water. On both my visits there was no previous ground baiting done. As this is such a wild fishery baiting a few days prior to your visit could set you up for a good day's bream fishing. I haven't fished Derrylough for pike but wouldn't be surprised if this lake holds some specimen fish. If you are in the area call round and give it a try.

How to get there
Approaching Arvagh town from the Longford road, you drive straight up as far as the T-junction with Foster's chemist shop straight in front. Take the right turn here and keep going for 0.3 of a mile and then keep left. Go on for a further 0.3 of a mile where you should also take the left turn. After another 0.45 of a mile you meet a junction. Turn left here and head out the Killeshandra road. You keep going for 3.55 miles and then take the left turn at the crossroads. Drive up this road for 1.7 miles and take the right turn there. Keep going for 0.2 of a mile and then turn right, take this road for 0.8 of a mile and then turn right down the narrow lane you meet there. The lake is at the end of this lane. There was work being carried out on the house just beside the lake on my last visit. **Do not forget to ask at the house for permission to fish.** Tight Lines.

Lough Aghnacor (12)

This lake or pond is definitely for the exploring angler. There is no shore fishing to be had on Lough Aghnacor. In fact, its shoreline is quite dangerous as I found out when exploring it for the purposes of this book. The lake itself is nearly weeded over with lilypads.

Verdict

The very soft banks are quite treacherous. You could quite easily sink down to your waist in soft mud. A rubber dinghy is the only possible way to fish Aghnacor. I always find it interesting to know what lies in these unfished waterways. This mystery is the only thing Lough Aghnacor has to offer the visiting angler!

How to get there

Approaching Arvagh town from the Longford road, you drive straight up as far as the T-junction with Foster's chemist shop straight in front. Here you take the right turn. Keep going for 0.3 of a mile and then keep left. Go on for a further 0.3 of a mile where you should also take the left turn. After another 0.45 of a mile, you meet a junction. Turn left here and head out the Killeshandra road. You keep going for 3.55 miles and then take the right turn at the crossroads. Continue here for 0.3 of a mile and then you can park at the two-storey house on your left. Go through the first gate on the right side of the road. In the field keep right and you will see alder trees surrounding the lake. Best of luck and be very careful.

Lough Drumkilroosk (13)

A rarely fished lake, Drumkilroosk is another one of those wild fisheries. A real gem for the exploring angler. The lake lies in scenic surroundings. I have no reports about this fishery. However, that old fisherman's feeling tells me Drum-

kilroosk could offer up some nice bream and tench fishing.

A fishery for the exploring angler. Drumkilroosk is rarely if ever fished. Note the newly planted rows of trees on the way down to the lake.

Verdict

If you are in the area do call round to Drumkilroosk; I have a feeling your visit will be well rewarded. I have never fished the lake, but Paddy and I are looking forward to discovering its mysteries. Out from the shoreline the lake is clear and easily fished. If you manage to fish Drumkilroosk let me know how you got on.

How to get there

Approaching Arvagh town from the Longford road, you drive straight up as far as the T-junction with Foster's chemist shop straight in front. Take the right turn here and keep going for 0.3 of a mile and then keep left. Go on for a further 0.3 of a mile where you should also take the left turn. After another 0.45 of a mile, you meet a junction. Turn left here and head out the Killeshandra road. You keep going for 3.55 miles and then take the right turn at the crossroads. Drive up this road for 0.65 of a mile and park on the right. You must walk up the road for about 100 metres, where you go in at the gate on your left. Go in at the gate and walk along rough ground to where you meet an ash tree. Turn into your left at this point, and walk about ten metres before turning right. Keep along the hedge for about twenty metres. At this point turn into your right and walk a few metres before turning into your left. You will now see the lake lying down in the valley. On my visit, the field on the way down to the lake was newly planted with small trees. If you make the effort, please let me know how you got on.

Lough Drumbess (14)

We are now visiting a small fishery that lies adjacent to the roadway. Lough Drumbess is a mystery to me. I haven't fished it and have no reports to pass on. When I visited the lake for the purposes of this book, there was a young goose patrolling the fishery. There is easy shore fishing beside the roadway.

Verdict

Once again, if you want to satisfy your curiosity then by all means pay Drumbess a visit. You should have no difficulties finding out what mysteries this small lake holds.

How to get there

Approaching Arvagh town from the Longford road. You drive straight up as far as the T-junction with Foster's chemist shop straight in front. Turn right here and

keep going for 0.3 of a mile and then keep left. Go on for a further 0.3 of a mile where you should also take the left turn. After another 0.45 of a mile, you meet a junction. Turn left here and head out the Killeshandra road. You keep going for 4.55 miles and then take the right turn. Go up this road for 0.3 of a mile and keep right at the junction in the road. Go along for a further 0.65 of a mile and turn left down a narrow road. Go on down here for 0.2 of a mile and you will see the entrance to the lake on your right. I wonder is that goose still patrolling the lake?

Mill Lough (15)

A noted pike fishery Mill Lough (or as it is often called locally Lough Portaliffe) is well worth a visit. It is a delightful scenic lake with a small island situated almost in the centre. I have fished Mill Lough on just a few occasions. I had some nice bream and Paddy landed a 16lb pike but reckons there are bigger fish lurking in this rarely fished waterway.

Verdict
When in these parts call around to Mill Lough. A local farmer told me about German anglers who regularly visit this lake for pike fishing. There is a small wooded area at the edge of the shore where rocks protrude out onto the lake. You will see this from the area where you shore-fish. I must find my way out onto this rocky ledge. Also some day I must visit the island in my rubber dinghy *Explorer*. I have a feeling this area could offer up some good fishing.

A view down to the small island on this picturesque fishery.

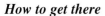

How to get there

Approaching Arvagh town from the Longford road, you drive straight up as far as the T-junction with Foster's chemist shop straight in front. Turn right here and keep going for 0.3 of a mile and then keep left. Go on for a further 0.3 of a mile where you should also take the left turn. After another 0.45 of a mile, you meet a junction. Turn left here and head out the Killeshandra road. You keep going for 5.9 miles where at the dangerous bend in the road you will see a gate on your right into the lake. This is a good area for launching a dinghy. There is no shore fishing here. For shore fishing you keep going for 0.45 of a mile and turn right. Go up this road for 0.45 of a mile and park at the old sheds on the left where there is a gate on your right. When you go through this gate, keep right until you see a small concrete pump house down to your left at the edge of the lake. Keep right of this pump house for shore fishing, also when you go through the gate you can head straight down the field and into the wood which brings you to the rocky outledge at the side of the lake. Tight Lines.

Lough Gartinardress (16)

Our final lake in the Breffni Quarter is Lough Gartinardress. On my first visit to this fishery I checked out the shoreline nearest the road, and could find no suitable shore fishing. It looked very promising, and I was going to report it as a lake for the exploring angler. However, on my next visit when I was filming the lake for my new video, I noticed what looked like a wooden stand over near

the wooded area. When the opporunity arose, I returned to Lough Gartinardress to check it out.

Another exciting looking fishery. You might just see the wooden stand on the far shore.

There was a gateway leading down through the woods so I decided to investigate this area. After a bit of searching, I discovered not one but three well built wooden platforms on Gartinardress. There were no signs informing the visiting angler and I would say because of this the lake is rarely fished. This looks like a very promising fishery, and I am mad keen to return for a day's fishing.

Verdict

Because of the pressure, I am under to complete this book and research my third book, I would say my opportunity to fish Gartinardress will be some time in the future. I have a feeling this is a top class fishery, so if you get the time to fish it please let me know how you got on. Photo on page 111.

How to get there

Approaching Arvagh town from the Longford road, you drive straight up as far as the T-junction with Foster's chemist shop straight in front. Turn right here and keep going for 0.3 of a mile and then keep left. Go on for a further 0.3 of a mile where you should also take the left turn. After another 0.45 of a mile, you meet a Y-junction. Turn right here and head out the Cavan road. From here you keep going for 5.3 miles and take a left. Continue up this road for 1.0 mile and pull in at the gate on your left. On my visit this gate was locked. There is an entrance to the right of the gate. To get to the wooden stands, you must walk along the laneway for 240 metres where you will meet a Y-junction. Keep right here and walk for another twelve metres. At this point you turn right into the wood and head straight down through the wood to the lake, where you will find the first stand. To get to stands 2 and 3, you keep up to your left and cross a wooden bridge. I found the water more weed-free at these stands. Best of Luck.

A lovely mirror carp from Derek Rowley's Lakeland Fisheries.

THE YELLOW SALLY - TIMES GONE BY
THE BLACKHEAD WORM

May 30th 1994 leaves pleasant, if somewhat nostalgic, images in my memory. It was my 44th birthday. I was doing a bit of weeding out in the garden when my wife Philomena called, "Paddy's on the phone, something about the mayfly on the Camlin". I hurried to the phone, "Paddy what's this about the mayfly?".

"Can't talk too loud. I'm here in the pub. There are two lads over in the corner chatting and I overheard one of them saying there was a good rise of mayfly on the Camlin up at Carriglass Bridge. They also said there were a few nice fish rising and they were planning to head up tomorrow evening. I have a few too many on me now or I would head up myself." "OK, Paddy thanks for the information I'll give it a try and let you know later how things worked out".

It must have been at least three years since I last fished this stretch of the Camlin. However, from past experience I knew the mayfly hatch would be at its peak between 6.00pm and 8.00pm. There would also be a smaller hatch of yellow sallies. It was a lovely mild evening with a slack wind – ideal dry fly fishing conditions.

I pulled my car into the gate on the right just up from Carriglass Bridge and proceeded up stream. I have found this stretch to be the most productive. As I approached the river, I could see flies hatching from the water and plenty of them in the air. Sure enough, there was also a scattering of yellow sallies floating down stream.

I proceeded to set up my fly rod and started to wander up river. The first fish I spotted was in near my own bank. As I studied the rise closer I noticed he was letting the mayflies pass and concentrating on the yellow sallies. As I had tied on the artificial may fly I decided to wait and see would the trout change his mind and take one of the may flies which outnumbered the yellow sallies by about 20 to 1. After about five minutes of close study it was clear this trout was adamant that the only meal he was interested in was the yellow sally.

As there's no point in flogging a dead horse I changed over to the artificial yellow sally. My first cast was spot on, about a yard in front of the fish. Not waiting for the fly to come to him the trout immediately moved up to intercept and I was in. The battle was short but intense before I finally brought the trout to the net. A lovely wild brownie of about three quarters of a pound.

With a heightened sense of confidence I proceeded upstream. The next fish to show posed somewhat of a problem. He was rising under the outstretched branches of an old ash tree and again feeding exclusively on the yellow sally. After a lot of thought I decided the best strategy was to approach as near as possible to the trout, without coming into his window of vision. This meant I had to crawl along close to the ground. This is the type of trout fishing I really enjoy, where the angler has to use all his watercraft to fool the rising fish into taking his dry fly.

When I had managed to get to within about eight yards of the trout I set about landing my fly a few yards up stream of the rise and allowing the line and fly to float down under the branches. Once again my aim was spot on and as the yellow sally floated over the trout, up he came and I was once more doing battle with a nice plump brownie. This time I had a bit of negotiating to do before finally landing a fish of just over the one pound mark. Of all the types of fishing that I have enjoyed over the years, I must confess that dry fly fishing for trout on a river brings me immense satisfaction.

With a nice brace in my bag I was feeling really chuffed with myself and looking forward to my next encounter. I hadn't to wait too long – up ahead about forty yards I thought I saw a slight ripple on the surface. This was a cause for further investigation. I moved up to within about ten yards of the spot and kept a close watch for any tell tale signs of a feeding trout. It must have been about ten minutes before the trout finally betrayed his presence. The signs were very subtle just a tiny ring on the surface as first a mayfly disappeared and a moment later a yellow sally met the same fate. From experience I knew this was a good fish and I would have to be at my best, if I was to deceive him.

River trout from around 3lbs and upwards are extremely wary when they are feeding on the surface. A bad cast, drag on the line or fly, a shadow on the water or sudden movement can easily put them down. So once again it was a case of down on all fours as I edged to within casting distance. Whenever I am about to

cover a good fish I seem to get that little bit nervous. Often it can prove just enough to upset my casting and so it was on this occasion. My fly landed right on top of the fish. As it floated behind him I was ready to lift the fly off the water when up he came and I could feel the hook making slight contact before the trout turned away and disappeared to the bottom.

That was the end of that. The only consolation I could learn from my experience was the fact that I now knew where a good trout resided. I guessed that he was definitely up around the 4lb mark and possibly heavier. As I often do in these situations I marked out the spot with a short length of stick pushed into the river bank. Whenever I returned to the river I would be able to locate my lost fish.

With my confidence now dented I made my way further up river. Here and there small trout were making their presence felt as they splashed madly about at what was now a mass of spent mayflies that were floating down on the river surface – laying their eggs as they travelled along and ensuring the survival of the species. About a mile from the main bridge where I parked my car, there is a small wooden bridge over the Camlin. Here I usually encounter a decent trout. On this occasion it came up trumps again. Right over at the far bank about a yard down from the bridge a nice brownie was steadily feeding. This fish wasn't so Catholic in its tastes and was gorging himself on both mayflies and yellow sallies.

To present my fly properly to the trout I would need to land it slightly under the bridge. This would call for some tricky casting on my part and after my previous experience my confidence wasn't exactly sky high.

However you never know what you can do until you try and as Paddy would say "You're not finished when you lose, you're finished when you quit". So I steadied myself and after a few false casts I finally took my chance. As the fly was about to land under the bridge the hook caught the edge of the outer plank and took a good hold. My response to this debacle is best kept out of print!

What next? At least the trout was paying no regards to my predicament. His own aim was a lot better than mine as he kept up a continuous onslaught on any fly that came his way. Could I turn failure into victory? A thought crossed my mind. What would Paddy do in this situation? If only I had a mobile phone to ring him and ask his advice. I decided to try and restore my confidence. Once again it was down on all fours as I crept up towards the bridge. At the bridge I decided to

crawl across on my tummy to the fly, hopefully without the trout being aware of what was going on. I could release the fly onto the water and make my way back to the rod and retrieve the situation.

As I was nearing the fly there was a small hole in the bridge through which I could observe my trout feeding away on the mayflies. To me he looked to be between 1.5 to 2lbs. I slowly reached my hand over to the fly and released it onto the water, immediately the trout swam up and hit the artificial with an almighty thump. This aggressive behaviour proved his downfall for in the process he managed to hook himself. It was now time for quick action as I speedily returned to my rod. Was he still on? The answer was yes.

As I played the fish he moved downriver for about fifteen yards. Eventually his fighting spirit gave way and I managed to slide him over the net. He was definitely a pound and a half and possibly more. With three nice trout to my credit I decided to take a rest under the shade of an old beech tree. As I was sitting there my mind started to drift back to times gone by. This stretch of the Camlin holds fond memories for me. It was here that I learned the art of dry fly fishing almost thirty years earlier, when Paddy spent what seemed like endless hours showing me how to stalk the trout as well as the importance of patience – not rushing into anything, waiting until the fly line had unfolded fully behind me and the importance of wrist action in presenting the fly to the rising trout.

In those days we had to cycle out to Carriglass. It wasn't all fly fishing – spinning and worming took up a large part of our time. Fly fishing was mainly confined to those couple of weeks when the may fly was up. In the early part of the season, spinning the Mepps or Lane Minnow proved the most successful, with some nice trout up to 6lb falling to those methods. Overall, I can honestly say that the blackhead worm was the most productive over the course of the season.

I remember those early days when Longford was a small quiet town where everybody knew everybody. On our way to Carriglass we had to pass by the travelling community who at that time lived in tents along a roadside that saw very little in the way of traffic. There was an almost timeless atmosphere. The hustle and bustle of modern times seemed to be absent. The call of the corncrake from the meadows was a constant reminder that modern agricultural methods still hadn't caught up with Ireland. In fact the last corncrake I heard was about twelve years ago in the fields along this very stretch of the Camlin.

One memory of that time that remains clear is when Paddy encountered a trout of about 2lbs, which was rising to the mayfly. The fish was feeding right under the branches of an alder tree, which were so low to the river that presenting a fly was impossible. "That's a clever trout, no hope of catching him," I said. Paddy was quick to reply; "There's a solution to every problem". After a bit of thought he removed his wellingtons and socks, and then proceeded to pull up the legs of his trousers. "Are you going to swim after him?" I said. "Don't get smart" was Paddy's reply and with that he took out a piece of cork and a single hook which he baited with a blackhead worm.

Paddy went upriver of the fish and waded across to the far bank. When he was nicely positioned, he allowed free line to the cork, which floated down under the branches. The worm was only about six inches from the float. As the cork made its way down river there was a slight boil on the surface where it disappeared. Paddy's reaction was immediate as he sank the hook home. This was Paddy at his best. Ingenuity, creativity and above all "you're not finished when you lose, you're finished when you quit".

Time was getting on and I had my birthday celebrations with Paddy in our local to look forward to, so I decided to call it a day and head back. When I arrived home that evening I was eager to tell Paddy all about my day's fishing and of course, the thoughts of a pint of stout was also high on the agenda. After a quick hello to my wife and a change of clothes it was back into my local where Paddy was deep in conversation with two of the competitors.

As if by instinct, he was first to turn around. It only took a quick nod and a wink for Paddy to know I had been investigating the information he had given me earlier in the day. With that Paddy ordered me a pint. After a while he said he would meet me in the toilet for a quick chat.

"Well, any luck?" Paddy asked. "Good evening's work, caught three nice trout on the yellow sally. Brilliant stuff. I also made a bit of a boob with a much larger trout." "Nerves got you. What do you reckon he weighed?" asked Paddy. "Over 4lb," I replied. "Good fish – did you mark him?" "Yeah I left the usual stick in the riverbank about a half mile up from Carriglass Bridge."

As it was my birthday Paddy showed his usual generous ways and treated me to a great night's craic and the two in the corner joined in. The next day around two o'clock the phone rang. It was Paddy. "Remember that good fish you marked?" My head sunk, I knew what was coming up. "He weighed in at 5lbs 12ozs, a lovely deep bodied wild brownie. He couldn't resist one of my blackhead worms," said Paddy.

Gently the water flows – this is the bridge over the River Camlin which I accidentally hooked, before eventually fooling that nice brownie.

Native Wild Brown Trout

I have huge admiration and respect for our native wild brown trout, who, over the years, have given me tremendous sporting memories.

Less than a mile on either side of my house, there are two small tributaries of the River Camlin, which are extremely important spawning areas for Lough Ree trout. One is the upper reaches of the Fallon, and the other we call the Dash River which runs under the road at Stonepark School.

Over the years I have kept a close watch on these two small rivers. They have in general been excellent nurseries for the young trout to grow up in. Pollution is by far the biggest threat to these small streams especially during late summer when water levels are running low.

Nature has placed a huge burden on our wild brown trout who must travel up these small tributaries to spawn. In recent times the Fishery Board and local angling clubs have become more aware of the trout's predicament, and are actively working to make those small streams more suitable for spawning and keeping a close watch out for pollution.

Lough Ree Trout Hatchery

One notable development in recent years has been the establishment of the Lough Ree Trout Hatchery in Athlone, Co. Westmeath. This is a voluntary organisation which does trojan work in the protection of our native wild brown trout.

Members are drawn from clubs in the Lough Ree catchment area. Every autumn, when the wild brown trout start to make their way from Lough Ree and up the small tributaries to spawn, the various clubs in conjunction with the Shannon Fishery Board trap a certain amount of both cock and hen fish. These trout are stripped of their milt and eggs which are then fertilised.

The eggs are transferred to the hatchery where they are grown on to young fry. In the hatchery the survival rate is very high – anything up to 90% while in the wild 20% would be exceptional. When big enough, the various clubs collect the

119

young trout and distribute them into the small tributaries in their area. The benefit of this work is now beginning to bear fruit, with our small tributary streams teaming with trout. Lough Ree is also benefiting enormously from this project and is coming back to its former glory days, when it was regarded as one of the finest wild brown trout fisheries in Europe.

The Poem

Back in the early 1980s as P.R.O. with the Co. Longford Angler's Club, I used to write a weekly column in both local newspapers on various angling matters in the county.

At the time, with the advent of intensive farming and inadequate sewage treatment plants, the wild trout stocks in our small streams were under the threat of extinction. I remember feeling a sense of anger and sadness at the plight of this great sporting fish so I decided to put my studies of the Lough Ree trout's life cycle into verse. This is a humble attempt on my part to honour this noble fish, and hopefully you might gain the same respect and actively work to ensure the survival of our native wild brown trout.

I first started this poem back about 1982 when I wrote a few verses. It's now 2004 and I have finally finished it. The poem depicts the Lough Ree trout's life cycle from an egg sheltering in the gravel of a small stream, to its early stages as a young fish finding its way in its new environment, its journey back downstream to Lough Ree, the various adventures in this vast habitat and its return spawning journey back to that little stream.

Bernie Murphy

POEM
Life Cycle – Lough Ree Trout
by Bernie Murphy

Noble fish of the watery domain; Among the gravel life first began
Egg, sheltering beneath the stones; Resting there till the rising sun
Surviving foes mainly three; Crayfish, dipper, slippery eel.

Life emerges to spring time's calling; For our young trout its all beginning
Wee fish of innocents and youth; Dart about in your tiny brook
Skills to learn to survive; Instinct your only guide.

Time to feed, what to do; Eye each morsel, could it be food
Helpless nymph in the current's grip; First taste of food for our wee fish
Time to search each rock and crevice; Nature's bounty it now increases
Nymphs, shrimp, waterlouse and caddis; All now part of your daily diet.

Sweet nymph of the stream; Time to rise take to wing
Dance about in sheer delight; As you perform your courting flight
Life's renewal with love's embrace; Must return – eggs to lay
Dancing there above the stream; Falling flat with outstretched wings.

Watching from his window view; Our young trout sees something new
On the surface overhead; Dying fly – eggs to shed
Have no time to inspect; Must quickly rise to intercept.

Summer sky clear and blue; Our young trout – something new
Drought threatens his little brook; Our wee fish knows what to do
Falling back to deeper water; New dangers lurk pike, perch and the otter.

Wriggling worm in the current's flow; Caution now as you move close
Hunger will decide your fate; Grabbing at this meal to taste
All's not what it seems; Must fight for life in that little stream
Fooled by the angler's bait; In his hands lies your fate
Mercy shown by the kind fisherman; Returns our trout, to its watery domain.

Springtime floods bring new awakening; Far away rich feeding grounds are waiting
Instincts urge must leave your stream; To Lough Ree you start to swim
Best to travel with dark of night; Avoid the jaws of the hungry pike
Other dangers on the way; Angler's bait, the poachers snare
Otter, mink, two more foes; But on your journey you must go.

New domain – you meet at last; Oh Lough Ree – so deep and vast
Fellow travellers you encounter; All one aim – satisfy the hunger
Feeding now on smaller fish; Weight you start to put on quick
No more wee fish of the stream; Now feared hunter of your new domain.

Summer enters as spring time fades; Time to change from the nymphal stage
Two years the lake bed spent; Time to rise for the mayfly nymph
Floating to the surface film; Breaking free fly to freedom
Rest a while one more change; Before returning from where you came.

Nature's bounty food galore; Time to move to Pollagh shore
Feast awaits in your window view; So many may fly, so much food
Feed away you noble trout; But beware, the angler's hook.

Summer sun high and bright; Brings discomfort to your eyes
Must retreat, find deeper shade; Venture forth at close of day
To feed again along the shore; With moths and sedges to the fore.

Autumn leaves like teardrops fall; Time to answer nature's call
Instinct urges you back home; To that little stream where life began
Return journey you must now go; Same old dangers, same old foes.

Travelling back through Shannon waters; In search of home where Camlin enters
Have no time to rest or feed; Must push on to make that redd
Scent of home your nostril brings; As you approach that little stream.

Excitement grows as you forge upstream; To that gravel bed where life began
With mate shimmering at your side; Eggs you lay now must hide
Flick your tail, it's all you need; Make that gravel bed into your redd.
Now protected lies your eggs; Back to Lough Ree it's time to head
Leaving life's renewal to start again; For those noble fish of the watery domain.

Top 5 Lakes

Since the publication of my first book, I have received numerous e-mails enquiring about tench fishing which seems to be very popular, particularly among British anglers. I have also received a lot of enquires about suitable lakes for the disabled angler.

In this book I have decided to include these two new categories to my top five lakes. I will also be including the old reliables from Book 1, Shore fishing, The Exploring Angler, Pike and Bream. As you travel around to fish the various lakes in both the Ten Stepping Stones and the Breffni Quarter, no doubt you will come to your own opinion. For now you can use my choice of lakes as a guide to get you started.

The following is the order in which we will be visiting each category in my top five lakes:
1. The Disabled Angler
2. Shore Fishing
3. The Exploring Angler
4. Top 5 Pike Lakes
5. Top 5 Bream Lakes
6. Top 5 Tench Lakes

Due to the inclusion of these two new sections, I have decided to change the format from Book 1, where I picked a different fishery for each category. In this book I will be including some lakes in more than one category.

Top 5 Lakes for The Disabled Angler

It was an e-mail from a British angler by the name of Chas Tarry which made me decide to include this category for disabled anglers. Chas pays regular visits to Ireland with a disabled friend and is always on the look out for suitable fisheries. He explained to me some of the problems facing disabled anglers – stiles, fences, marshy ground, long distances to the shoreline, etc.

As I thought through the fifty-two fisheries in this book, I could only think of one – Lough Errill, where access has been made easy for the disabled or

wheelchair angler. Hopefully in the future more thought will be put into the building of wooden platforms so they are constructed to make access easy for the visiting disabled angler.

I hope the following five fisheries which I have chosen in this category are suitable for the needs of the disabled or wheelchair angler and will allow them to enjoy a good day's fishing. However, if they are in any way unsuitable I would be delighted to hear from you.

We will be visiting two lakes in the Ten Stepping Stones – Loughs Errill and Sallagh. With three from the Breffni Quarter – Loughs Cullie, Rockfield and Glasshouse.

Lough Errill

For our first lake in this category we travel to Lough Errill, *No. 5 in the Ten Stepping Stones.* Of all the fisheries in this book, Errill has a well built wooden platform only a short distance from the parking area and easily mounted by the disabled or wheelchair angler.

The one disadvantage with the lake is weed growth, which is very prevalent in the summer months. Errill can also be a hard water to have success on. The fish are there but it can be tough work getting them into your swim. This is a noted tench fishery.

Report and Directions on pages 26 and 27.

Photos on pages 26 and 80.   Tight Lines!

Lough Sallagh (2)

Next, we venture over to Lough Sallagh. This is the second Sallagh Lake, *No. 20 in the Ten Stepping Stones.* Fortunately for the disabled angler, besides offering up easy access, Sallagh is also a top class coarse fishery and I would highly recommend it. When you meet the lake there is the possibility of shore fishing beside the amenity area, however, if you drive further on for around 0.3

of a mile you will meet a pass into the lake on your left. This part of the shore offers up easy fishing into weed-free water and you can park right beside the lake.

Report directions and story on pages 43 and 46.
Photo on pages 43, 70 and 73.
Best of luck with those big bream!

Cullies Lough

For our third lake we visit Cullies Lough, *No. 2 in the Breffni Quarter.* Like Lough Sallagh, I have written a story about my first visit to Cullies Lough.

Another delightful fishery. When you meet the lake there is plenty of parking place. Access is right beside the parking area. This part of the lake is a noted hot spot for tench. Fishing is into twelve to sixteen feet of water, which is mainly weed-free. You can drive right down to the lakeshore.

Report story and directions on pages 92 and 97.
Photo on page 92.

Lough Rockfield

Our fourth fishery in this category is Lough Rockfield, *No. 6 in the Breffni Quarter.* When you drive down to the end of the steep lane you will find easy shore fishing at the edge of the lake. At this point you will be fishing into sixteen to twenty feet of weed-free water.

For more shore fishing you can drive into your left at the Alder Avenue Drive along to the gaps in the trees on your right and pick a suitable spot. Along this shore you will be fishing into between 14 to 18 feet of water, which is weed-free.

Report and directions to Rockfield on page 101.
Photo on page 74.   Tight Lines!

Glasshouse Lough

We are now visiting our final lake in this category, Glasshouse Lough is *No. 8 in the Breffni Quarter,* I have not fished this lake however from reports I've heard from British anglers, it seems Glasshouse is a quality coarse fishery. You can drive along the side of the lake where there is easy access to comfortable shore fishing. I would highly recommend this fishery for the disabled angler. The visiting angler will be fishing into water which is weed-free.
Report and directions on pages 103 and 104.
Photo on page 103.

Top 5 Lakes for Shorefishing

I suppose one could say this category is for the elderly angler who enjoys his fishing but cannot venture as far as he used to, the leisure angler who puts his comfort as his top priority and of course the angler who is always short on time and looking for somewhere easy to fish. For these types of anglers besides the ease and the comfort, a net full of fish is also well received. The previous five fisheries for the disabled angler would also be suitable for this category. However, I am going to pick five new ones that are a little more difficult to access but can still be classified as comfortable lakes for shore fishing.

The first four fisheries, Loughs Gortinty, McHugh, Tully, Hollybank, are from the Ten Stepping Stones while the final lake Corlisbratten is from the Breffni Quarter.

Gortinty Lough

This fishery lies right beside the main N4 road. You can drive down to the gate at the edge of the lake. When you cross this gate you are right beside loads of easy shore fishing, which is into eight to ten foot of weed-free water.

Gortinty is the first lake we visited in this book and is the ideal fishery for the angler who is short on time.
Report and directions on pages 21 and 22.
Photo on pages 22 and 76.

Lough McHugh

Our second lake in this category is Lough McHugh. You can drive down close to the shore of this fishery where you will find plenty of parking place.

About twenty meters from the parking area there's a wooden stand. You will also find plenty of easy shore fishing along this side of the lake. You will be fishing into six to ten feet of water which is weed-free.

I have a feeling Lough McHugh could be a top class coarse fishery. I have not fished the lake myself but I am really looking forward to paying it a visit.

Report and Direction on Page 25.
Photo below and also on pages 25 and 73.

Brian Bohan on the upper shore of Lough McHugh.
Inset – note the deep body of this McHugh bream.

Tully Lough

For the angler looking for an easy day's fishing then Tully Lough is just the lake. You can drive right down to the shore where there is easy fishing, in fact, if it's wet you could fish out the window of your car!

For loads more easy shore fishing there's a small wooden stile on your left. If you cross this stile you have all the easiest shore fishing you could want and it's into eight to ten foot of weed-free water.

Full report and directions on pages 54 and 55.
Photo on page 54.

Lough Lower or Hollybank

Hollybank is another gem of a lake for easy shore fishing. I would highly recommend this fishery particularly if you are part of a group of anglers.

You will find loads of easy shore fishing into weed-free water. At the parking area you must cross a small wooden stile. When you cross the stile walk up the field for about 100 metres and turn left into the shore of the lake.

If you decide to visit Hollybank, I have a feeling you will have made a good choice. This lake is *No 36 in the Ten Stepping Stones.*

Report and direction to Hollybank are on pages 64 and 65.
Photos on pages 64 and 77.   Best of luck!

Lough Corlisbratten

My final lake in this category is Corlisbratten, *No. 4 in the Breffni Quarter.* This is a delightful little fishery.

During 2003 there was a lot of work done along the shore of the lake, which has left it easily approachable. Corlisbratten lies only a short distance from the road.

There are plenty of wooden stands on the lake, which also offers up easy shore fishing. If you want a nice little comfortable fishery, then Corlisbratten is for you.

Full report and Directions page 99.
Photo on page 99.

Top 5 Lakes for exploring angler

Hidden and mysterious – two words I would use to describe the following five gems for the exploring angler. I must admit I find this a fascinating category. Wondering what lies below the surface of these wild fisheries is a delight in itself.

The following five lakes are rarely if ever fished mainly because of the difficulty in getting to them and also the fact that few people know about their location. This is definitely a journey for the angler who wants to go where few anglers have gone before.

We will be visiting three lakes in the Ten Stepping Stones – Loughs Clooncose, Doogary, Mullandaragh, and two in the Breffni Quarter – Dernaweel and Drumkilroosk.

Lough Clooncose

No matter how much I tried, I honestly couldn't find shorefishing on this lake. From the photo on page 82, it's there somewhere. If you manage to find it, I hope you bag up like never before.

A rubber dingy would be ideal to explore Clooncose. Fortunately the lake lies only a short journey down one field. For the angler who makes the effort I have a feeling he could be well rewarded with some top class fishing.

Clooncose is unfishable from most of its very weedy and soft shoreline. A river runs out of the neighbouring lake, Fearglass, and into Clooncose so I presume this fishery holds much the same species. Clooncose is *No. 22 in the Ten Stepping Stones.*

Full Report and Directions on Page 48.
Photo on Pages 48 and 82.

Lough Doogary

Another mysterious fishery Lough Doogary lies only a short distance as the crow flies from Clooncose. The river that enters Clooncose from Fearglass runs on down to Doogary.

Like Clooncose a rubber dingy would be the best way to explore Doogary. This lake lies a long way down the fields. I have that old fisherman's feeling Doogary could be an exciting fishery. It was heavily overgrown with lily pads when I paid it a visit for the purposes of this book and also to do some videoing.

In early spring you might get some shore fishing before the lilies start to grow. Doogary is *No. 24 in the Ten Stepping Stones.*

Full Report and Directions on Pages 50 and 51.
Photo on Pages 50 and 76, also front cover.

Peter Dillon outside his pub and guesthouse, the Pikeman's Inn. It was by a chance encounter with Peter that I found out about Tony Egan's fabulous catch of bream on Doogary. Peter has a great knowledge of the lakes around the Ballinamuck area. If you are in this part of the Irish Midlands do call around to Peter's traditional Irish pub, and you might meet up with that other knowledgeable angler, Tony Egan.

For more information you can log into his website at **www.dillonspub.com** or email **pikeman@eircom.net** Phone: **043-24137**. Outside Ireland **00-353-43-24137**.

Local Knowledge

They say when it comes to fishing, you can't beat local knowledge. The following two anglers – Brian Bohan and Tony Egan are as good as you will get. So if you are visiting this part of the Irish Midlands and you would like to have a swim picked out in advance for your favourite type of fishing or maybe you would like the convenience of a pre-baited swim, a day's boat fishing for pike, or just up-to-date information – then you can contact Brian by phone at home on 07196-31870; mobile 087-4124851 and Tony on his mobile 086-3493044.

Lough Mullandaragh

This fishery is *No. 32 in the Ten Stepping Stones.* It was in Mullandaragh during 2001 when I spotted my last otter. Mullandaragh offers up only a small amount of weedy shore fishing. The real secret of this fishery will be found out by the angler with a rubber dingy.

The only report I have is from a local farmer who told me Mullandaragh holds some nice pike and bream. I have earmarked this fishery for an early morning's fishing in my rubber dingy *Explorer* and to do some videoing. I also hope to encounter that otter.

Full Report and Directions on Page 60.
Photo on Page 60.

Lough Dernaweel

The fourth fishery in this exciting category is Lough Dernaweel. This is a truly mysterious lake and a real gem for the exploring angler. It will mean a long hike down the fields to get to the lake, however I have a feeling the effort will be well rewarded.

Dernaweel offers us only a small amount of shore fishing, a rubber dingy would be the ideal way to explore it. Dernaweel is a very picturesque lake that's crying out to be fished. If you get there before me please let me know how you got on and the best of luck. Dernaweel is *No. 5 in the Breffni Quarter.*

Full Report and Directions on Page 100.
Photo on Page 74.

Lough Drumkilroosk

Our final lake for the exploring angler is Lough Drumkilroosk. Hidden away in a valley, thankfully this fishery offers up plenty of easy shore fishing.

The problem with Drumkilroosk is getting to the lake. The visiting angler will have to negotiate some very rough land. However I have a feeling the effort will be worthwhile.

I would say this lake is rarely fished. On a visit for the purposes of this book and also on a visit the following year to do some videoing, I could find no evidence of the lake being fished.

I am going to stick my neck out once again and say that I think this could be a nice bream and tench fishery. If you want to find out Drumkilroosk is *No. 13 in the Breffni Quarter.*

Full Report and Directions on Pages 108 and 109.
Photo o n Page 108.
Best of Luck

Top 5 Pike Lakes

As I sit down to write these notes its early March 2004, here in the Irish Midlands, the weather over the past few weeks has been lovely and sunny with crisp frosty morning's ideal piking conditions.

Pike fishing is becoming very popular here in Ireland, with more and more anglers pursuing this side of the sport. On a recent visit to Corby, in Northamptonshire England, I met up with some local anglers who told me that pike fishing is also a popular sport in Britain and how they love to visit Ireland in pursuit of *esox*.

For the five lakes that I have chosen in this category I have kept both the boat and the shore angler in mind. Boat fishing for pike is extremely popular and the angler visiting any one of these five fisheries will quite easily be able to launch an 18ft boat.

We will be visiting four lakes from the Ten Stepping Stones – Loughs Cloonfinnan, Rinn, Gulladoo, and I am including three for the price of one with The Three Sisters Lakes. The lone representative from the Breffni Quarter is Lough Rockfield.

Lough Cloonfinnan

Our first visit is to Lough Cloonfinnan, *No. 6 in the Ten Stepping Stones.* This is a small shallow lake that can be a problem with weed growth, however I have a feeling there are large pike in this fishery.

If you decide to visit Cloonfinnan, then late winter and early spring when weed growth is not such a problem are the best times. A float fished or ledgered dead roach would be the ideal method on this shallow fishery.

My best pike from Cloonfinnan weighed in at 15lbs 3ozs, and was caught on a float-fished dead roach. Paddy has taken some nice fish up to the 14lb mark, however don't be surprised if you encounter 20lb plus pike in this delightful coarse fishery.

Full Report and Directions on Pages 27 and 28.
Photos on Pages 28, 70, 73, 84 and back cover.

Lough Rinn

Our next visit brings us to Lough Rinn, the largest lake in this part of the Irish Midlands. You could divide Rinn Lough into two sections, the upper half from Rinn House to the amenity area is quite shallow, only going down to a depth of between four to six feet and below Rinn House where the lake gets much deeper reaching a depth of twenty-four feet.

For the pike angler in pursuit of really large pike the deeper section of the lake could be your best bet, however you can expect to encounter specimen pike throughout this delightful fishery.

Rinn Lough is *No. 13 in the Ten Stepping Stones*. At the amenity area you will find easy access to launch a boat. Around to the left just below Rinn House you will come into a bay. On the far shore of this bay a small river runs into Lough Rinn from Errew Lake. If you want you can negotiate the short journey up this river into Errew where you can enjoy some more good pike fishing.

Full Report and Directions on Pages 34 and 35.
Photos on Pages 34, and 35.

The Three Sisters Lakes

We are now getting three lakes for the price of one. The Three Sisters Lakes *No's 26, 27 and 28 in the Ten Stepping Stones* are all easily negotiable by boat via a small river, and offer up delightful pike fishing.

As I said in my earlier reports on these three fisheries they are ideal for the angler planning a weekend's fishing-cum-camping-holiday. Loughs Gortermone, Tully and Beaghmore offer up plenty of shore fishing, while on both Gortermone and Tully you will find an easy boat launching area.

The pike angler can expect to encounter specimen fish in either of the Three Sister Lakes, and I would highly recommend them for a visit.

Full Report and Directions on Pages 52 to 56.
Photos on Pages 52, 54, 56 and front cover.

Gulladoo Upper and Lower

Gulladoo is quite a large lake system that is divided in two by a short stretch of river. This is a top class pike fishery and I would highly recommend it for a visit.

When you drive in towards the folk park, you will find an easy boat launching area on your left at the lower part of the lake. This section of Gulladoo offers up nice pike fishing. I have found the bottom half of the lake over to the right the most productive. The pike angler will also find plenty of easy shore fishing along lower Gulladoo.

To get to upper Gulladoo, you will have to bring your boat up the river and under the bridge. Upper Gulladoo is deeper than the lower section going down to a depth

of forty feet. This part of the lake can throw up large specimen pike. It also offers up plenty of easy shore fishing. Gulladoo is *No. 31 in the Ten Stepping Stones.*

Full Report and Directions on Page 59.
Photo on Page 59.

Lough Rockfield

Our final lake in this category is Lough Rockfield, *No. 6 in the Breffni Quarter.* When you drive down the steep hill to the shore you can launch a boat at this area. Rockfield also offers up plenty of easy shore fishing.

This is another delightful pike fishery. Rockfield varies considerably in depth. Up to the right from the boat launching area the lake gets very shallow going to a depth of only two to four feet, while in the middle of the lake, you will find a depth of over forty feet. Up to the left where a small river enters, the average depth is between four to seven feet.

This small river runs down from Drumhart Lake, and if you want you could make the journey by boat up to Drumhart where you could find some more nice pike fishing. There is also a river that leaves Rockfield, along the far shore and up to the left. This river runs down to Glasshouse. I have never been down this way. If it is possible to get to Glasshouse via this river, then you could enjoy some more pike fishing. I would recommend Rockfield for a day's pike fishing. This fishery is reported to hold some large brown trout.

Full Report and Directions on Page 101.
Photo on Page 74.

Joe McDermott with this 18 pound pike, taken on a dead roach from the Shannon just below Tarmonbarry Falls. This was during the spring of 2004.

Thoughts on Catching Wild Irish Bream

Elusive, mysterious and a joy to catch, wild Irish bream are high on the agenda with visiting coarse anglers.

Bream are a shoal fish. When the angler encounters one there are usually plenty more in the vicinity. I have found the bream shoals feed more actively when water temperatures are fairly high. This is usually during the months of June, July, August and September.

During these warm summer months, about one hour before nightfall the bream shoals start to move out of their daytime resting areas to feed nearer to the shallows. The bream feed most actively for the next two hours, after which they seem to take it easy before starting to feed actively again during the hour before daybreak until one hour after before moving back to the deeper water to rest up during the daytime.

I have often wondered why at this time of the year, wild Irish bream do not feed more actively during the daylight hours. I presume, and the following is only guesswork on my part that the bream who are large slow moving fish, would prove easy prey for pike, and so prefer to move about and feed during darkness when they are less likely to be seen by the resident pike population. Another possibility could be that the bream's natural food supply of nymphs, shrimps, snails etc, are more active during the late evening and early morning. It could also be a combination of these two factors, or maybe even some other reasons unknown to me.

Having found out the best time of day and also the year when wild Irish bream feed more actively, the next problem facing the visiting angler to a wild Irish lake is where to locate the bream shoals. You could be lucky enough to pick a swim where the bream are feeding or move into during your stay. However the best bet is to heavily ground-feed your swim with your intended hook bait for as many days prior to your fishing trips as possible.

Summing up

Finally to sum up, I am going to pass on these three tips to help the visiting coarse angler to catch more of those deep bodied wild Irish bream.

Best Time of Year

The warmer summer months – June, July, August and September when water temperatures are usually at their highest.

Best Time of Day

One hour before sunset – one hour after.
One hour before sunrise – one hour after.

Best Method to locate Bream Shoals

Groundbaiting, groundbaiting and even more groundbaiting with your intended hook bait as often as you can prior to your fishing trip. This is the best method to entice the bream shoals into your chosen swim.

Top 5 Bream Lakes

After passing on some of my thoughts on catching wild Irish bream, I am now moving on to my top five bream lakes. I have chosen four from the Ten Stepping Stones – Loughs McHugh, Cloonfinnan Sallagh and Hollybank, while the one representative from the Breffni Quarter is Lough Rockfield.

Out of the five I have had good bream sessions on Cloonfinnan, Sallagh, Hollybank and Rockfield. I have not fished McHugh, however on a visit for the purposes of this book, my fish-finder showed up a lot of large fish present in this delightful fishery, which I presume were bream shoals.

Lough McHugh

Someday, God willing, I must have a day's fishing on this delightful fishery. From reports I have heard from visiting anglers, Lough McHugh, *No. 4 in the Ten Stepping Stones* seems to be a good bream fishery.

With a total of four wooden stands and loads of easy shore fishing, McHugh offers up plenty of comfort for the visiting angler. Of all the lakes in this book that I have visited with my fish finder McHugh held by far the largest concentration of fish, with loads of big fish also showing up.

If you get the chance to fish Lough McHugh I would be delighted if you would pass me on information about your day's fishing. Bernie.

Full Report and Directions on Page 25.
Photo on Pages 25, 73 and 127. Tight Lines.

Lough Cloonfinnan

First let me say Cloonfinnan can be a difficult fishery to have success on. I have recommended Cloonfinnan to various anglers, only to find out they had a poor day's fishing.

There are some fabulous bream in this lake as can be seen in photo on page 70. These fish were taken during a morning's session. There were two anglers accompanying this British angler. They were only about fifty metres apart, however his two friends caught no bream. Could it be a bream shoal moved into his swim? Or maybe they were lying up resting in this part of the lake?

I was delighted to get this photo as evidence of the quality of bream in Lough Cloonfinnan. The swim where this angler caught his bream is 100 metres up to the right of the pass way as you face the lake. Cloonfinnan is *No. 6 in the Ten Stepping Stones*.

Full Report and Directions on Pages 27 and 28.
Photo on pages 28, 70, 73, 84 and back cover. Tight Lines!

Lough Sallagh

We are now visiting a first class bream fishery. Lough Sallagh is *No. 20 in the Ten Stepping Stones* and holds good stocks of bream. If you can get in loads of ground-baiting for a good few days prior to your fishing visit, then you can expect good sport to those wild Irish bream. Sallagh is easily accessible and although it can be very weedy in places, the shoreline along by the roadway is usually clear of weeds.

Early morning or late evening is when you can expect to bag up on this lovely little fishery. Hopefully you will hit upon the same sort of bream fishing that Paddy and I enjoyed on our first visit to Sallagh all those years ago.

Full Report and Directions on Page 43 and 46.
Photos on pages 43, 70 and 73. Tight Lines.

Hollybank or Lower Lough

Known locally as Hollybank, this fishery has loads and loads of comfortable shore fishing. On a recent visit in July of 2004, I met up with some anglers who were having a great bream session on Hollybank. Ledgering maggot between thirty to forty metres out was the successful tactic.

Hollybank is another delightful fishery and a joy to fish – all that comfortable shore fishing into weed-free water makes this a must for the shortlist. Hollybank is *No. 36 in the Ten Stepping Stones* and the final fishery in Area 3.

Full Report and Directions on Pages 64 and 65.
Photo on pages 64 and 77. Tight Lines.

Lough Rockfield

Lough Rockfield, *No. 6 in the Breffni Quarter* is quite a large lake. Hitting on the bream shoals can be difficult. However if you do get them into your swim, expect a hectic fishing session.

There is something peaceful about this fishery. I can't put my finger on what it is, maybe the way the little inlets along the Alder Avenue bring you out to the lake shore, or the way Rockfield is tucked away down in a valley.

I was talking to a local farmer who told me about the bream shoals which congregate along the shallow bay up to the right of Rockfield as you meet the lake. He told me they visit this area during the springtime. I presume this must be the part of the lake where they spawn.

Full Report and Directions on page 101.
Photo on page 74. Best of Luck.

My Top 5 Tench Lakes

Tench – shy and secretive. Since the publication of my first book I have received numerous e-mails, phone calls and letters from anglers enquiring about good tench fisheries here in the Irish Midlands.

I could see by their enquiries that most of these anglers were in fact specialist tench fishermen. Their knowledge not alone of the fish but also of the various techniques used to catch them, were far in advance of anything that I knew. Over the years the tench that I have caught were usually part of a mixed bag. Except for pike I have never really concentrated on any one particular coarse fish species. I have always been content with whichever type of fish happened to venture into my swim. Having said that, the capture of a tench was always a highlight during my fishing trip.

Out of the fifty-two fisheries in this book, the five that I have chosen for this chapter will hopefully be suitable for the needs of the tench angler. These are Aduff, Cloonfinnan, Drumbad, Gortermone, all from Area 3 and the Royal Canal.

You might be wondering why I included the Royal Canal. I have decided to give a treat to the dedicated tench angler, and bring him forward to my fifth book, when I will be covering this fishery. The Royal Canal is proving to be a real Mecca for visiting tench anglers. With the help of Mullingar-based tackle dealer David O'Malley, I will be letting you into some of the secrets of this record-breaking tench fishery.

Lough Aduff

I am starting off with a fishery that I have not fished myself. However, I have received plenty of good reports by visiting anglers about the tench fishing on Aduff – *No. 2 in the Ten Stepping Stones.*

From my enquiries it seems the best part of Aduff for tench is up to the left as you meet the lake. The best overall fishing method is a combination of maggot and worm ledgered about thirty metres out. Very early morning sessions seem to prove most successful with plenty of previous ground baiting.

There are plenty of wooden stands situated along the shoreline, which allows for an easy day's fishing.

Full report and directions on page 23.
Photos on pages 23 and 77.

Lough Cloonfinnan

Without doubt, probably one of the finest tench fisheries in the Irish Midlands, as can be seen from the photo on the back page.

Cloonfinnan – *No. 6 in the Ten Stepping Stones* – is a must for the serious tench angler. It only goes down to a depth of between four and five feet and can be heavily weeded in places. Brian Bohan's catch of twenty-eight tench was taken from the shore at the drive-in area. This is the only really clear bit of bank on the lake. The successful method was ledgering a maggot and worm combination about thirty to forty metres out. Brian had done almost a week's ground baiting prior to his visit.

One bit of caution – Cloonfinnan, like a lot of the fisheries in this area, can be a hard water to have success on. So remember ground-baiting and even more ground-baiting of your intended hook bait prior to your fishing visit.

Full report and directions on pages 27 and 28.
Photos on pages 28, 70, 73, 84 and back page.

Lough Drumbad or Clooncoe

Another top class tench fishery, Drumbad is a record breaking tench lake. Of all the lakes in this area, for some reason, Drumbad consistently throws up the largest tench.

In places this fishery can become very weedy. However, if you keep well up to the left you will have a better chance of weed-free water. Once again, I would highly recommend this lake for the serious tench angler.

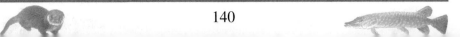

140

If you are visiting this area, put Clooncoe or, as it is known locally, Drumbad on your short list, and if you enjoy rudd fishing then there will be an extra bonus waiting for you. Drumbad is *No. 17 in the Ten Stepping Stones.*

Full report and directions on pages 39 and 40.
Photos on pages 39, 40 and 77.

Lough Gortermone

For some reason, in recent years Gortermone has come on in leaps and bounds as a serious tench fishery. This is good news for the tench angler who can also enjoy plenty of easy shore fishing.

Another tench lake for the short list, Gortermone, is a real comfort to fish with plenty of weed-free water. The worm and maggot combination on a size 12 hook fished on the bottom about thirty to forty metres out usually proves the most successful.

This is the first of the three sister lakes, and proves by far the best for tench. Why this should be I do not know, however, whatever the reason, it's a good tench fishery for the visiting angler. Gortermone is *No. 26 in the Ten Stepping Stones.*

Full report and directions on pages 52 and 53.
Photos on page 52 and front page.

Royal Canal

I am now bringing you forward to Book 5 when I will be writing about this fabulous tench fishery. The reason is because of all the enquiries I have received looking for information on the Royal Canal.

As a tench fishery, the Royal Canal is up there among the best in the Irish Midlands. You just have to look at the photos of David O'Malley's catches on the Canal, near Mullingar, to see the quality of tench this water holds.

Beside Mullingar town a unique event occurs on the Royal Canal – its otherwise stagnant water becomes rejuvenated with crystal clear limestone water. This water enters the Canal via a small river that runs out of Lough Owel. I don't fully understand the effects this limestone water has on the Canal, but one obvious change is to make the water crystal clear and continually on the move – similar to a limestone river.

This environment produces big tench, as can be seen in the photos on page 69. In fact, David O'Malley broke the Irish record during 2002, with a 9lbs 3ozs tench taken on sweetcorn. However, he did not enter the fish for the record books. As there is no report or directions to the hot spots on the Royal Canal in this book, the best advice I can give you is to call around to David O'Malley at his fishing shop in Dominic Street, Mullingar. David is very helpful and is the best bet in getting tips on baits, methods and directions. You could also log into John Cole's excellent website **www.innyangling.net** where you will find information on both the Royal Canal and the River Inny.

Irish Record and Specimen Weights

Since my first book, when I gave the Irish Record and Specimen Weights for 2001, there has been only three changes in the listings for 2003.

The river-caught pike record has been broken as well as the roach and roach-bream hybrid records. What has surprised me is the pike (lake) and tench records are still intact. With the amount of pike fishing and the explosion in tench fishing particularly on the Royal Canal, I am surprised these two records have managed to hold out.

In the following run-down of the various Record and Specimen weights for 2003, I am going to include carp which are becoming more and more popular among coarse anglers.

Pike
Record Lake: 41lbs, Ian Wortley, Lough Ross, Crossmaglen, Feb. 2002.
Record River: 42lbs, M. Watkins, River Barrow, March 1964.
Specimen Weights: Lake: 30lbs.   River: 20lbs.

Tench
Record: 8lbs 1.5ozs, Nick Parry, Ballyeighter Lake, June 1995.
Specimen Weight: 6lbs.

Bream
Record: 12lbs 3ozs, Paul Mathers, Bolganard Lake, May 1997.
Specimen Weight: 7lbs 8ozs.

Perch
Record: 5lbs 8ozs, S. Drum, Lough Erne, 1946.
Specimen Weight: 3lbs.

Eel
Record: 6lbs 15ozs, John Murnane, Droumanisa Lough, June 1979.
Specimen Weight: 3lbs.

Roach
Record: 1.425kg, Terry Jackson, Drumacriten Lake, October 2002.
Specimen Weight: 2lbs.

Rudd
Record: 4lbs 8ozs, Hugh Gough, Coney Lake, September 1996.
Specimen Weight: 2lbs 2.5ozs.

Rudd-Bream Hybrids
Record: 7lbs 10ozs, Brendan Doran, Monalty Lake, October 1996.
Specimen Weight: 3lbs.

Roach-Bream Hybrids
Record: 7lbs, Roy Gretton, River Banne, Toome, April 2002.
Specimen Weight: 3lbs 8ozs.

Carp
Record: 29lbs 13ozs, Sidney Kennedy, The Lough, Cork, July 1998.
Specimen Weight: 12lbs.

The two Ronnies from Essex in England, fishing the Royal Canal at Abbeyshrule. The nearest Ronnie is 81 years young, while his companion is 71.

John Harvey
1938 – 2003

Thanks for the Memories

Trip to the Moy – Pork shanks on Lough Owel – Record pike on Lough Ree

Throughout my life, I have been fortunate to have met up with so many friendly and interesting anglers. This has added greatly to my fishing trips. Over that period of time one angler who became a very close friend was the late John Harvey.

Myself and John had a lot of things in common which included football, wild fowling, having a drink and fishing. In this area John's main interest was the pursuit of salmon, trout and pike. We have had many a memorable day's fishing together. The following is a short account of three fond memories of my fishing exploits with John over the years.

Trip to the Moy

It was back in the early nineteen eighties when our local club arranged a salmon fishing trip to the famous River Moy in County Mayo. Neither myself nor John had ever been salmon fishing and we were really looking forward to this trip.

The stretch of the Moy we were heading for was at the village of Foxford. On our arrival we couldn't wait to get onto the water. Our plan was to fish down stream with a bunch of blackhead worms and then spin back up stream with Toby's and Devon minnow.

John headed off downstream in front of me searching out likely lies with his bunch of worms. As is often the case on my first trip to a new fishery I like to observe for any information that might improve my knowledge of both the water

and the method that proves successful. Just below the bridge in Foxford, I met up with a local who was fishing a method new to me. It was a plastic bubble float with a team of three wet flies attached. He was using the bubble float both as a weight to cast his flies and also to help with hooking a fish. While I was observing, he took two nice sea trout with this method.

John's voice rang out, "Bernie I'm into a fish" I hurried down to John only to find he had taken a small eel. As we rambled on down stream, I observed another angler fishing a bubble float. I called to John to point out the method this angler was using, as we watched John said quietly, "Bernie I can't see any flies or bait attached to the float."

We decided to move closer and observe. I could see the angler was very wary of our presence. His first comment was to ask us where we were from. When we told him we were part of a visiting group of anglers from Longford, he noticeably relaxed. After chatting for a while it became clear we had met up with one of the local poachers.

The poacher offered us a demonstration in the art of snatching salmon. This is a method where a weighted treble hook is cast into a likely salmon lie, the poacher then snatches the treble hooks up through the water hoping to fowl hook a salmon.

This was a very experienced poacher. He knew the river like the back of his hand. Pointing out a protruding stone he said "There's usually a nice salmon lying just down stream of that rock".

He removed the bubble float, which was used as a decoy. He then tied on a large treble hook with a lump of heavy lead attached to give it extra weight. His cast was just downstream of the rock when the treble hook found the bed of the river. He slowly reeled in line until he had a direct contact with the treble hook.

The poacher waited on for a while telling us the disturbance caused by the treble hook would have moved the salmon and it would be a few moments before he returned to his lie. With that, he made a powerful snatching movement with the hooks forcing up through the water. His first attempt was successful as he hooked a good-sized salmon. At this stage the poacher forced the fish ashore with his heavy line and rod.

When the salmon was safely landed the poacher whistled out and a man suddenly appeared from behind a hill at the side of the river. He was an accomplice whose job was to collect the salmon and bring him to a waiting car which was parked close by. This was the first salmon we had seen caught even if it was by foul means.

Myself and John fished on without success. Situated on the corner in the town just up from the river is a pub, I think it's called the Angler's Rest. John had noticed this ale house before we had set off fishing as a sort of insurance policy in case the fishing was poor. "Bernie I'm thirsty, do you think we should head back to the pub for a break and a quick one?" said John. I readily accepted the offer. Salmon fishing can be very tiring and trying pursuit when you are having no success. If my memory serves me right out of our party of over twenty anglers, Ballymahon man John Heneghan was the only one to catch a salmon – taking two grilse on wet flies.

When we entered the pub three of our club members had found their way there before us. Joe Carr, Martin Malone and the late Brian Harkin were sitting up at the counter enjoying their pints. I knew this was the end of my first day's salmon fishing. Sometime later the bus driver was blowing his horn furiously outside the pub. When we arrived back in Longford our first port of call was The Market Bar before we finally ended up in John's favourite alehouse The Lyon's Den. It was well into the early hours before a taxi was called to bring myself and John home.

Pork Shanks on Lough Owel

Lough Owel is a large crystal clear limestone lake situated just outside Mullingar in County Westmeath. The lake is spring feed and has very little in the way of natural spawning streams. To keep up trout stocks the Fishery Board have to introduce farm-reared trout. The first introduction of these fish usually takes place around May.

For the early spring months the visiting anglers are in pursuit of trout, which have over wintered, and could now be classified as wild fish. It was during the early spring months when John and I would do most of our fishing on Owel. This consisted of a small amount of wet fly fishing, however, most of our time

was taking up with trolling lane minnows and rappallas behind John's boat. With water temperatures at this time of year on the low side, the fly life of the lake is usually sparse and the trout have to concentrate mainly on the shoals of small fish fry. It was these trout that myself and John were after. Trolling a bait behind a boat can become very boring if you're not meeting fish, however, when a trout does take it is usually with an aggressive thump that causes great excitement in the boat.

Looking back now there were two seasons when I really looked forward to my trips with John to Lough Owl. At the time one of John's sons worked in a local pork factory from where he used to bring home cooked pork shanks. I remember well the first time John brought one along. We were out fishing near Church Island when he said it was time to pull in for a bit to eat. We parked the boat on the sheltered side of the island and dropped anchor. I took out my usual sandwiches and soup. John was busy searching the bottom of his bag before producing a pork shank.

I could get the lovely smell. "Do you like pork shanks"? he asked. I remarked that they were very tasty and with that John produced a second shank, which he gave to me. On that rather cold spring day I can tell you John's offer was greatly appreciated. There is something special about the break for a bite to eat while out fishing. All kinds of things are talked about and it usually builds up a good bond between the anglers. After that day for the following two seasons when John's son was working in the pork factory we would always make a point of stopping off at Church Island for a bit of a rest, a good chat and of course those tasty pork shanks.

Record Pike on Lough Ree

It was early on a Saturday morning during the summer of 1995 when John phoned me, "Bernie would you like to come for day's pike fishing on Lough Ree?", he asked. The night before that John had met up with his friend Seamus Finn who told him he was welcome to use his boat for a day's fishing. Seamus's boat was parked along the shore of Lough Ree up at Saint's Island.

I readily accepted John's offer. We headed off around midday. Our plan was to troll artificial baits behind the boat. We were in pursuit of big pike, which this

part of Lough Ree is famous for. Lough Ree is a large lake and in windy conditions can be very treacherous. However, on this particular day the winds were light. John brought along his engine and did the driving. We drove from Saints Island keeping close to the shoreline; it wasn't long before we started to encounter pike. I took a fish of around 4lb on my plug bait. John was fishing a 2-inch rappalla and having great sport with big perch.

We encountered a few more small pike before John decided to drive over towards the far shoreline. On our way, there was plenty of banter going on between the two of us, when suddenly John's rod hit a fish. Thinking it was another small pike John, who was working the engine, asked me to play the fish. At the time I thought the pike wasn't too big maybe, around 6lb to 8lb. However, when the fish came to within about twelve metres of the boat the rod bent over viciously as the pike turned and swam in a different direction. "We're onto a good one here", I called to John.

It seems that while I was playing the pike he was swimming directly towards the boat and not putting much strain on the rod, but as soon as he changed direction I knew I was onto a good fish. We must have spent the best part of thirty minutes playing the pike as my arms got tired. John took over the battle. Lucky enough he'd brought along his extra large home-made landing net, which we managed to get up over the pike before hauling him into the boat.

In the past I have seen pike that weighed close to the 30lb mark and I can honestly say that this fish was far heavier. Could he have been a record sized pike? On the day we had no scales or camera with us. The temptation to bring him ashore and get him weighed entered our minds, however, the pike's welfare was paramount and we decided to release him back into the lake, where if he is still swimming around today he must surely be over the 50lb mark.

It was a joy to be in John's company he was friendly, cheerful and ever willing to put himself out so other people could enjoy themselves.

Cheers John and thanks for the memories.

Coming up in Book 3

IT IS now 19th August 2004, I am sitting here by my window looking out at the rain and thinking to myself, how am I going to sort out Area 5 and Area 6 in Book 3?

At my last count, there were 76 lakes to visit – no doubt when I start to study the areas more closely I will find even more. To be perfectly honest, out of the 76 fisheries I have only fished about half a dozen. This part of the Irish Midlands has been neglected on my part. Why, I do not know. Maybe it's because of all the top class coarse fisheries in both Book 1 and Book 2.

There are two large lakes – Lough Gowna in Area 5 and Lough Derravarragh in Area 6. I could quite easily write a book about these two fabulous coarse fisheries. However, I have taken up the challenge and as soon as this book is finished, I will be off in my trusty Suzuki Jeep to visit all 76 lakes for Book 3.

I plan to fish as many lakes as possible. I also hope to meet up with some local anglers who might be able to give me some up-to-date information on the various fisheries. This local information is invaluable as was proved by Brian Bohan and Tony Egan in Book 2. If you, the reader, happen to fish any of the lakes, I would be grateful if you would pass on any information on fish species present, depths, successful fishing methods and baits, photos, etc. I have mapped out Areas 5 and 6 on next page, so you will know where the lakes are situated.

In Book 3, I will be including all the old favourites from Books 1 and 2. There will be plenty of photos, plus stories of times gone by, and no doubt on my travels through Book 3 I will have some new adventures to write about. I have some new ideas about restocking and the Fishery Board, which I think will be of benefit to both the coarse angler and the Fishery Board. I hope to have a chat with some of the tourist interests to see if they have any plans for the improvement of angling here in the Irish Midlands. I would also love to meet up with the people in government who have responsibility for coarse angling and hear what their plans are.

So there you have it, Book 3 with all those 76 lakes will be my biggest challenge to date, especially as over 90% of them are still a total mystery to me. However, I am looking forward to the challenge, and hope to drag Paddy along on some of the fishing trips.

NOTE:

I plan to give a page on my website over to the progress of Book 3. I hope to start in November 2004, when hopefully the publication of this book is out of the way. If you would like to read about my travels and adventures in Book 3 when I boldly go where probably no angler has gone before, then log into **www.berniemurphy.com**

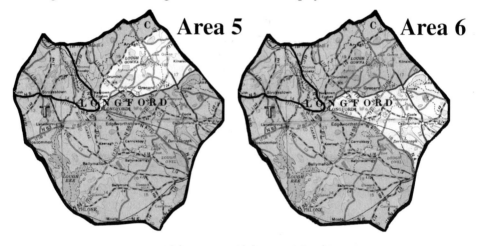

Final Thoughts

WE ARE at that stage in the book where I take the opportunity to air some of my own personal thoughts on coarse fishing here in the Irish Midlands. As I did in Book 1, I will be giving these thoughts in the form of a wish list.

My first wish in Book 1 concerned funding for the Fishery Board. From reports I have heard, it seems the allocation of funding has not changed and the Fishery Boards are finding it very hard to make ends meet – so much so that there is talk of letting go some members of staff and there is often not being enough money available to put diesel in their lorries.

I think this is an awful insult. Not only to the Fishery Board members but also to anglers and the protection and maintenance of all those fabulous wild fisheries which Ireland is so famous for.

For my first wish, I would love to see both anglers and everybody with an interest in angling tourism to lobby their local TD in an effort to get a substantial increase in funding to the Fishery Boards.

My second wish concerns *Mr Pike* – I am so fond of this great sporting fish. Down the years I have enjoyed countless fishing trips in pursuit of *esox*. On many a cold frosty day, both myself and Paddy have headed off to our local river or lake for a day's piking. I love this time of the year when the air is fresh and wholesome, and *Jack Frost* is blanketing the countryside. With a flask of hot soup and some tasty sandwiches I could not think of a better way to fill in a cold winter's day.

For my second wish, I would love to see a new law coming in, where anglers are not allowed to kill any pike. At present an angler can take one pike home from his fishing trip which must be under 6lb in weight. The present law can quite easily be abused whereby a group of anglers can go on more than one fishing trip in the same day and bring home their allocation of pike a number of times. A complete ban on the killing of pike by anglers would put a stop to this.

My third and final wish concerns Lough Cloonfinnan, probably one of the finest wild coarse fisheries in Europe. Despite the fact that this fishery is packed with big bream and tench, it still takes an experienced angler to fool these wild Irish fish into taking their hook bait. There is one serious drawback for the visiting angler to Cloonfinnan – this concerns the shortage of shore fishing. Many an angler arrived at the lake only to find the small bit of shore fishing was taken up by other anglers.

For my third wish, I would like the Fishery Board to build a couple of wooden stands on this delightful fishery.

Cheers Bernie Murphy

Paddy: Bernie, I enjoyed that journey through Book 2.

Bernie: Paddy, I feel the same. We've encountered some fabulous fisheries.

Paddy: I was wondering about Book 3, and all those lakes you will have to visit.

Bernie: Book 3 is going to be a huge challenge. I'm hoping you will be able to help me out.

Paddy: Is this book now finished.

Bernie: Yes Paddy – Book 2 is at an end.

Paddy: Bernie, do you think it might be a good idea to head on down to the pub to discuss Book 3 over a wee drink?

Bernie: Good man Paddy!

Hope to meet you all again in Book 3.
Bye from Paddy and bye from me.

GONE FOR A PINT

BOOK 1

The Complete Guide to Coarse Fisheries in the Irish Midlands – Book 1

by Bernie Murphy

"I found the book an absorbing read. Bernie takes the reader on a fascinating journey to all 69 fishing locations in this part of the Irish Midlands. I can recommend this book both as a guide to angling in the Irish Midlands and an entertaining read."
— *Derek Rowley, Irish International coarse angler*

"An excellent pocket-sized book for the dedicated coarse angler. This is an essential book to have in the tackle box."
— *Frank Quigley, Angling Ireland Magazine*

"Bernie has fished the region for over 40 years and you could hardly have a more informed guide. He covers each venue in a relaxed, honest and personal way."
— *Garrett Purnell, Midland Angler (British Angling Magazine)*

"A resounding success … a lovely book, full of those delightful little anecdotes that only Irishmen can tell."
— *Jim Baxter, Angling Star (British Angling Magazine)*

SPECIAL OFFER
~~WAS €9.95 (£7.50 Sterling)~~
~~NOW ONLY €7.50 (£5.00 Sterling)~~

ALL BOOKS
€11.95

(includes postage and packaging)

To purchase, please send Cheque, Postal Order or Bank Draft to:
Bernie Murphy
CURRY, ATHLONE ROAD, LONGFORD, IRELAND
email: berniemurphy30@hotmail.com • website: www.berniemurphy.com
PROCEEDS GOING TO CHARITY

www.berniemurphy.com

BERNIE MURPHY'S FISHING SITE

WELCOME

I must apologise for the state my website was in. Thankfully, it is now well improved – I must thank Niall Gallagher, a friend of my daughter's husband for the improvement.

In future, I am hoping to include a monthly magazine, which will give readers up-to-date information on coarse fishing here in the Irish Midlands. I will be out and about checking on the lakes, taking photos and picking up useful tips. As the winter is now approaching, I hope to do a special feature on pursuit of winter pike.

The website is handy for me to keep you, the reader, in touch with all that's happening. For Book 3 I will let you know how it's progressing and also keep you up-to-date on my new video on Book 2 – which I am finding very exciting, as it shows all the lakes as well as some good action shots of anglers with their catches.

So, if you want to log in to the site — **www.berniemurphy.com** — I hope you will find something of interest. I would also welcome emails on ideas you might have for the improvement of the site or information you would like to read about.

Video of Book 2

At present I am working on a new video to complement Book 2. This video will give you, the reader, the opportunity of viewing in the comfort of your own home, each of the fifty-two fisheries in this book.

I will be showing the various approach routes, suitable areas for shore fishing, wooden stands and overall views of the lakes. There will also be some good action shots of anglers with their catches, plus tips on best methods and baits for the various lakes. In an effort to keep down costs, I have purchased my own video camera from the sales of Book 1. I am doing the videoing myself as well as the commentary.

So far, I am very pleased with the progress of the video, however, the real test will be how well it is received by fellow anglers. If there is anything that you might think would be of help to visiting anglers, I would be delighted to hear about it.

The proceeds from the video will also be going to my three charities – **Longford Hospice Home Care**, **Save the Otter** and **Our Lady's Hospital for Sick Children**.